BLACK WARRIORS:
THE RETURN OF THE BUFFALO SOLDIER

IVAN J. HOUSTON

BLACK WARRIORS: THE RETURN OF THE BUFFALO SOLDIER

iUniverse books may be ordered through booksellers or by contacting:

iUniverse
1663 Liberty Drive
Bloomington, IN 47403
www.iuniverse.com
844-349-9409

Because of the dynamic nature of the Internet, any web addresses or links contained in this book may have changed since publication and may no longer be valid. The views expressed in this work are solely those of the author and do not necessarily reflect the views of the publisher, and the publisher hereby disclaims any responsibility for them.

Any people depicted in stock imagery provided by Getty Images are models, and such images are being used for illustrative purposes only.
Certain stock imagery © Getty Images.

ISBN: 978-1-6632-5130-5 (sc)
ISBN: 978-1-6632-5133-6 (hc)
ISBN: 978-1-6632-5129-9 (e)

Library of Congress Control Number: 2023904288

Print information available on the last page.

iUniverse rev. date: 03/22/2023

INTRODUCTION

One million black Americans served in the armed forces during World War II. We were the laborers, the cooks, the orderlies, the messmen—not the fighters. Almost all of us were assigned to service units, driving trucks, building airfields, unloading ships, and other menial tasks. It was as if the South had won the Civil War. There were exceptions, and even some of the service units experienced heavy combat—for example, the "Red Ball Express," which supplied General Patton's tanks with fuel, and a battalion that flew barrage balloons, protecting the landings on D-Day. There were a few scattered tanks, tank destroyers, and artillery battalions that also saw some combat action.

After much political pressure from black leaders, the Ninety-Ninth Pursuit Squadron and later the 332nd Fighter Group commanded by Colonel Benjamin O. Davis Jr., a West Pointer (because of his race he was not talked to socially during his four years at West Point) and the son of the first black general, entered combat. These black aviators became the Tuskegee Airmen.

Meanwhile, black leaders and the black press, much stronger and much more vocal than today, kept up the pressure— "Send our boys to combat." This was not a hollow cry. It was felt that being in combat would help us attain first-class citizenship in our own country.

In 2005, some sixty years after the end of World War II, I started writing a book about my experiences as an infantryman in the last racially segregated infantry division to experience combat in our country's history. It was a unique experience. I thought it was a part of history that needed to be shared. I also made a few speeches about what happened to me.

My book, *Black Warriors: The Buffalo Soldiers of World War II*, was published in the spring of 2009. It was revised and reprinted in 2011. I've included a summary of that book in chapter 1 so that you have the necessary background for this book.

My returns to Italy and annual visits from 2012 to 2018 have been one of the highlights of my long life. I felt that I represented every World War II Buffalo Soldier, and I could see how the Italians of Tuscany looked at us as their heroes. We were the African American soldiers who gave them their freedom, and I have been delighted to learn more about them, experience their reenactments, and discover *Il Volto Santo*, the Holy Face of Lucca, when I least expected it. Each of the chapters from chapter 2 through chapter 7 contains photographs at their ends.

Ivan J. Houston
May 2019

PROLOGUE

Dad started writing this book a few years ago and finished most of it before his death on March 1, 2020. The Houston Family Trust, including myself and my sisters, Pam and Kathi, has completed what became Dad's final story. My sisters and I traveled to Italy with Dad many times. We worked closely with Dad on this and his previous book, *Black Warriors: The Buffalo Soldiers of World War II*, as well as on all of his media, social media, and acted as his support in appearances and book signings. The story is historical, topical, and personal, just like Dad.

Following the last chapter, we included an afterword with pictures and remarks from some of our Italian friends who were there with Dad on his initial and subsequent visits. Mattea (owner of Villa La Dogana), Flavio (reenactor), Marco (swimming coach), and Francesca (reenactor and hugger) all played roles in making Italy our dad's second home.

—Ivan Abbott Houston

CHAPTER 1

THE BACKSTORY

I completed my freshman year at the University of California at Berkeley and enlisted in the army the day before I turned eighteen. By enlisting, I was given a six-month deferment. I was called to active duty on January 3, 1944, and then reported for duty at Fort MacArthur, San Pedro, California. I was immediately segregated because the white recruits went one way, and we black recruits went the other way. After a few weeks of testing and learning the ways of the army, I was sent to the Army Specialized Training Program (ASTP) for infantry basic training at Fort Benning, Georgia.

Thirty of us recruits from Fort MacArthur were sent by train to Fort Benning. Emmett Chappelle and I were the only two black soldiers among the recruits. Because of that, we bunked together. We had both done well on our tests, and the army was sending us to this special program where we would get infantry training for thirteen weeks and then return to college in an accelerated program. After graduating, we would return to the army for active duty. It was another seventy years after infantry training at Fort Benning before I would hear again from Emmett. He was a famous NASA scientist with numerous patents and had read my book *Black Warriors: The Buffalo Soldiers of World War II.* Emmett's letter to me said, "So much of whom I became—and who I am now—was determined by my years as a Buffalo Soldier. Ivan, a great deal of African American experience is unknown, unrecorded, and lost. History is, after all, written by the victors. *Black Warriors* is a contribution of great value to revealing the truth." Emmett was inducted into the National Inventors Hall of Fame in 2007.

I also received a letter from Jim Tucker after my book was published. Jim and I were in the battalion's Intelligence Squad when we went to Italy. Jim was in another ASTP group, but we met at Fort Huachuca, Arizona. He was a great sprinter and scholar, receiving his PhD in economics, writing books on finance, and becoming the first African American officer of the Richmond Branch of the Federal Reserve Bank. He was the bank's senior vice president when he retired. Shortly after the war, one of his proudest moments was running and winning the 4 x 4 relay in Frankfurt, Germany. Despite a painful hamstring pull near the end of the race, Jim persevered, inspiring General George S. Patton, an avid track and field fan who witnessed the race, to remark that Jim was "one of the most courageous men I have ever met." On the troopship crossing the Atlantic Ocean, Jim and I talked about many things. One of our most frequent discussions was about the German army's general staff and how it worked. That was probably a strange discussion for two black privates, but when we arrived in Italy, we encountered one of the German army's greatest generals in Field Marshal Albert Kesselring.

During our voyage, Jim Tucker, McKinley Scott, George Gray, James E. Reid, and I played cards on deck during the day. Scott, Gray, and Reid were killed in action in the battles that were to come in Italy. Jim gave me some advice after the first printing of my book. He told me to put an index in *Black Warriors: The Buffalo Soldiers of World War II*, which I did for the second printing. Jim passed in 2016 at age ninety-one.

I was also contacted by the son of my company commander, Captain Hugh D. Shires. Shires was one of our white officers, and he was a very good leader. Shires's grandson, who had tours of duty in Afghanistan, found my book while doing research on the internet. Shires told his son before he passed away in 2007 that all the soldiers in the battalion made him very proud.

In March 1944, the army program I was assigned to was terminated, and all of us recruits, mostly young college students who scored high on the army's General Classification Test, were sent to infantry divisions—the invasion of Europe was pending, and infantry casualties were expected to be high.

We black ASTP soldiers—there were six of us in a company of two hundred—were sent to the racially segregated Ninety-Second "Buffalo" Infantry Division. (By the end of the war, I learned that of the six, two were killed in action, and Emmett and I were both wounded. I do not know what happened to the other two.) We were called Buffalo Soldiers because that was the insignia of the division—a black buffalo. After the Civil War, black soldiers were sent west to engage the Indians. The Indians called them Buffalo Soldiers because of their hair and because of their bravery.

The Ninety-Second Infantry Division was commanded by Major General Edward M. Almond, a Virginian. The higher line infantry officers—major and above—were all White and mostly from the South. (The army felt Southern white officers knew how to handle black soldiers.) Junior officers were both black and white, but when we entered combat, no black officer could ever command a white soldier or officer, regardless of rank! All enlisted men in the division were black. As an eighteen-year-old soldier, I did not give this much thought. This was the way the country and the military had been run since the birth of our nation.

I joined the Ninety-Second Division in March 1944 and was assigned to Headquarters Company, Third Battalion, 370th Infantry Regiment. I would remain in that company for the duration of the war, serving as a scout, as assistant to the operations sergeant, as battalion clerk, and finally as battalion sergeant major. Our operations sergeant, T. T. Davis, made us keep meticulous records on a minute-by-minute, hour-by-hour, day-by-day basis of everything that happened to our battalion while in combat. That record, the operations journal, became the basis of my first book, *Black Warriors: The Buffalo Soldiers of World War II.*

The home base of the Ninety-Second Infantry Division was Fort Huachuca. Fort Huachuca is in the southern Arizona desert near the Mexican border. There were no civilian communities anywhere near the fort. There were some fifteen thousand soldiers in the Ninety-Second Division. The largest units were three infantry regiments, the 365th, the 370th, and the 371st. There also were artillery, combat engineer, and medical battalions as a part of the division.

My regiment, the 370th Infantry, separated from the rest of the division in the spring of 1944. Along with the 598th Field Artillery Battalion, companies of combat engineers and medics, Combat Team 370, was formed. The buffalo insignia and anything identifying us as part of the Ninety-Second Infantry Division was removed from everything we carried. The late Leo Branton, a noted Los Angeles civil rights attorney, was in the Ninety-Second Division's Reconnaissance Unit at Fort Huachuca. Leo called me after he read my book and said, "I finally know what happened to the 370th. We all woke up one morning in July 1944, and the whole regiment was gone!"

As Regimental Combat Team 370, we left Fort Huachuca on July 1, 1944, and sailed from Hampton Roads, Virginia, on July 15, 1944. According to our regimental commander, Colonel Sherman, we were a select group of officers and men, and we often called ourselves "Sherman's Raiders." I had just turned age nineteen and frankly looked forward to a great adventure. Some of us shaved our heads so we would look fierce, like Native American warriors, as we got ready to face the Nazi Germany war machine.

There were four thousand Combat Team 370 soldiers on the troop transport, USS *Mariposa*. We sailed the Atlantic Ocean as a lone ship, not in a convoy. The nights were beautiful as all the stars in the sky looked like shimmering jewels. We arrived off the coast of North Africa in just over a week and then sailed through the Strait of Gibraltar, landing at Oran, Algeria, on July 24 for a very short stay. We transferred to the navy transport ship USS *General G. O. Squire* on July 26 and set sail for our next destination, Naples, Italy. We landed at the bombed-out port of Naples on August 1. The people we saw on our way to our encampment were begging and looked extremely destitute.

We stayed in Naples, encamped in an extinct volcano, for several days, and then the 854 soldiers of my Third Battalion left Naples on a small coastal steamship, the *John Jay*. We slept on deck for the short time it took us to get to the bombed-out port of Civitavecchia, which is north of Rome. We camped and trained until army trucks took us north about 150 miles to the front lines near Cascina, on the south side of the Arno River. The river was running low since it was the end of summer, and the banks were sandy, muddy, and devoid of all vegetation. It was August 23, 1944. The Germans were on the north side of the river. Looking out from a forward observation point, off in the distance I could see a very tall, round tower, and it was leaning just like it's described in the history books—one of the seven wonders of the world. It was the Leaning Tower of Pisa. To me, seeing one of the wonders of the world was unforgettable. Even from a distance, it was gleaming white and very majestic.

We sent patrols to determine if any of the enemy were still on the south side of the river. Patrol activity also needed to contact the allied units to our left and right. We were under the command of the First Armored Division. Finally, we were ordered to find the best place to cross the Arno River. On August 24, 1944, during one of these patrols, Sergeant James E. Reid, a friend I had played cards with during the crossing of the Atlantic, was killed, becoming the first black infantry soldier killed in combat in Europe during World War II.

On September 1, 1944, attached to the famous First Armored Division and often riding their tanks, we crossed the Arno River and liberated Pisa and many of the towns and villages in that part of Tuscany. The Japanese American One Hundredth Battalion attacked on our left flank. I encountered a Japanese American soldier near the tower in Pisa; we were both crouching down next to the very high wall that surrounded the tower complex as we tried to avoid sniper fire. The soldiers of the One Hundredth Battalion were Japanese Americans from Hawaii. They had not been put in relocation camps, and many had volunteered for army service. The One Hundredth Battalion, with about a thousand soldiers, later became part of the Japanese American 442nd Infantry Regiment, soldiers who all volunteered to fight for our country. They became the most decorated regiment in the United States Army.

It is interesting to note that the army force first crossing the Arno River was the white First Armored Division, the Japanese American One Hundredth Battalion, and the African American 370th Combat Team. In September 1944, I don't think anyone was aware of the historic fact of that diversity.

As we moved through the villages and towns on the north side of the Arno River, east of Pisa, hundreds of starving and cheering Italians surrounded our vehicles. They threw flowers at us and shouted, "Viva Americani." They had been behind German lines for months without adequate food. Except for a few Fascists, most of the people we encountered were truly happy to see us because they were now free! Celebrations in each community seemed to grow as the morning became night. At a hamlet just north of the Arno River, the citizens greeted us with cries of "Viva Americani" and "Buon giorno" and other phrases that were beyond our limited vocabulary. Others just waved happily. Some of the women and men were crying. The excited civilians clung to our vehicles and showered the soldiers with grapes, flowers, and fruit. Some ran alongside, pouring wine for all who would accept it, while others of both sexes and all ages paid their tribute with hearty kisses. They had every guy in the column feeling like a conquering hero. Even today, I smile and feel good when I recall those scenes. Here were white Italians greeting black Americans as liberators and showering us with love, while in our own country, we remained second-class in all respects.

Heavy fighting erupted along the front after we crossed the Arno River as we fought our way north toward the medieval, walled city of Lucca. On September 4, our regimental executive officer was killed, and we suffered heavy casualties as Company I, often riding on tanks, battled its way into the village of Ripafratta, near Lucca, in central Italy. Major Aubrey R. Biggs was the first white officer killed in action in our regiment.

My battalion was ordered to capture the fifteenth-century Villa Orsini, about five miles outside the city of Lucca. We accomplished this mission and established the villa as a stronghold point. The capture of Lucca and the Villa Orsini in early September 1944 was part of a fast-moving combat operation that was to have great significance in my life almost seventy years later.

In early October 1944, Combat Team 370 was given the assignment to capture Mount Cauala, a mountain that dominates the Ligurian plain, which would lead our armies to the cities of Masa and Carrara. Our First Battalion, suffering heavy casualties, was not able to make it to the top. First Lieutenant Alonzo M. Frazier, a black officer, was mortally wounded during the assault, and his battalion suffered many additional casualties. Frazier refused a medical corpsman's offer to take him to the rear. He continued to lead his platoon until he died. He now lies with four hundred other Buffalo Soldiers in the Florence American Cemetery and Memorial.

On October 12, the Third Battalion Rifle Companies I, K, and L crossed the river at the foot of the mountain and, using rope ladders, finally reached the top. They were immediately hit by German counterattacks and, after a series of these attacks, began to run out of ammunition. I volunteered with a dozen soldiers to try to get ammunition to the top of the mountain. Our ammunition patrol was bombarded by artillery fire from the very beginning. We lost several men as we tried to make it to the top. We never made it. Hot shrapnel fell and burned through my clothes. Our men at the top were overrun. As the battle raged, First Lieutenant Ralph Skinner, Company L, was seriously wounded. Lieutenant Skinner continued to lead his platoon but died of mortal wounds as the battle raged. Private Jake McInnes fired his Browning Automatic Rifle, killing and wounding several Germans. During the battle, McInnes was knocked out by a concussion grenade. He survived and was brought down the mountain. Both Lieutenant Skinner (posthumously) and Private McInnes were awarded the Silver Star for their gallant and heroic action. McInnes later returned to action.

My battalion was not able to hold on to Mount Cauala and finally fell back to the town at its base, Seravezza. The Third Battalion suffered many casualties in that terrible battle. Looking back, I'm certain I was temporarily shell shocked—or in today's terms, suffered from post-traumatic stress disorder (PTSD). My stomach was upset, and sometimes my hands would shake. I was awarded the Combat Infantryman Badge for exemplary conduct in action against the enemy for trying to get ammunition to the top of the mountain. I received a ten-dollars-a-month pay increase and when the war ended was awarded the Bronze Star Medal. My hands still shake when I think about that battle.

Much later, in fact while I was doing research for my book, I read we were severely criticized for our actions at Mount Cauala and Seravezza. The criticisms came from Fifth Army Headquarters because we did not hold on to our objective. This is hard to understand since we had to use rope ladders to climb the mountain and were continually bombarded by artillery and mortars. Machine guns raked our positions, and we finally ran out of ammunition. What more could we have done?

In December 1944, my battalion was moved about twenty miles to the east, north of Florence and Pistoia. We were deep in the Apennine Mountains and very soon deep in the snow. We were placed under the command of the Sixth South African Armored Division, a unit that fought with the British Eighth Army against German Field Marshal Erwin Rommel in the North African desert. Our front line was very quiet for almost two months. We were provided white winter uniforms. Today, it seems sort of unreal that black American soldiers; mostly from America's South, would be fighting in deep snow in the North Apennine Mountains under the command of South Africans. But that is the way it was.

During that very cold winter, the Germans often bombarded us with propaganda leaflets encouraging us to surrender. These pamphlets would show a photo of a black soldier who had been captured. But we weren't influenced by this propaganda. We kept fighting because no one wanted to be a prisoner of the Nazis.

On December 26, the Germans attacked elements of the 366th Infantry, which was another black regiment that had relieved us. The 366th Infantry was not a part of the Ninety-Second Infantry Division, but it was all black, including its senior officers. General Almond did not want them assigned to his division. He greeted them with such caustic remarks that Colonel Queen, their black commanding officer, became sick and had to be relieved. Almond told them that the only reason they were there was because the black press insisted that they see action. He said they would see action and would sustain their share of casualties. Their previous assignment had been to guard airfields throughout the Mediterranean. They probably were not ready for the harsh realities of infantry combat and indeed suffered heavy casualties. There are at least 113 soldiers of the

366th Infantry buried at the Florence American Cemetery, yet official army records show no casualties for this black American regiment. This remains a mystery even to this day.

A unit of the 366th was at the mountain village of Sommacolonia on December 26 when they were attacked by an overwhelming German force. They did fall back, but Lieutenant John Fox, seeing himself surrounded, called for artillery fire on his own position. He was killed along with several enemy soldiers. Lieutenant Fox was awarded the Distinguished Service Cross thirty-eight years after that action and the Medal of Honor in 1997. In World War II, only five artillery officers were awarded the Medal of Honor. Lieutenant John Fox, Cannon Company, 366th Infantry, was one of them.

In January 1945, my battalion was released by the South Africans and returned to the Ninety-Second Infantry Division. This was just in time to engage in another battle near Mount Cauala. On February 8, we were ordered to attack Hills X, Y, and Z—that was the name given to these unidentified hills by higher command. They were on the western side of the mountain.

We were the only attacking division in the US Fifth Army at that time. Much later, I read that General Almond wanted us to keep the Germans busy so they would not be able to relieve their forces on the Russian front.

The attack was a disaster. Many officers and enlisted men were killed or wounded during that failed offensive, including two of our rifle company commanders. Captain Clarence Brown, the company commander of L Company, was wounded and became shell shocked. Lieutenant Reuben Horner, our battalion's most decorated soldier, received his third Purple Heart for wounds to go along with two Silver Star

Medals and three Bronze Star Medals. Captain Jessie Jarman, the company commander of I Company, was killed. Captain Jarman looked like a kid and wore his captain's bars highly polished, even in combat. Perhaps that led to his death in this action. Posthumously he received the Silver Star and the Bronze Star Medals for his heroic actions.

Our situation in this battle was aggravated when we were bombed and strafed by our own airplanes. I was with Company K, and one of our own US P-47 fighters strafed our position several times. Some of our soldiers took off their shirts to show they were black, but the strafing continued.

Part of the 366th Infantry Regiment was ordered to attack the German positions where the Cinquale Canal flows into the Ligurian Sea. They were attacking with tanks, and the tanks became stuck in the sand. A very heavy German artillery barrage hit the attacking forces, and they suffered very heavy casualties. The attack failed, and this black regiment was decommissioned within a month, and its surviving personnel were sent to service units.

Captain Brown, the shell-shocked commanding officer of Company L, came into the battalion command post. He cursed out everybody present before he was sent to the hospital. Every one of his platoon leaders, black officers, had been wounded in this battle. I later learned that Captain Brown was killed in action in the Korean conflict. He was a very hard-nosed and gruff commander and was respected by his men.

As a result of the February battle, the Ninety-Second Division was completely reorganized. All companies in the 370th Infantry were sent white commanding officers. Fifty-two officers and 1,264 enlisted men were transferred to other regiments in the division from the 370th Infantry. The 370th

Infantry received replacements from other regiments who were considered combat reliable. This happened because there were no trained black enlisted infantrymen available for the Ninety-Second Division. We could not accept white replacements because they would have to serve under black commissioned and noncommissioned officers, and that was against army policy. The other two regiments of the Ninety-Second Division, the 365th and the 371st, were stripped of their best enlisted men, and they were sent to my regiment, the 370th.

Our final attack came in April 1945. We crossed the Cinquale Canal, the western anchor of the Gothic Line of fortifications. During this attack, I was blown through a door by mortar fire as we occupied a large villa. My back was stinging, and a small piece of shrapnel was stuck in my shoulder. I was treated by Doc Young, our battalion medical officer, and sent back to battle with a very sore shoulder. I was later given the Purple Heart Medal for wounds received in combat.

As we moved forward in this final attack, Lieutenant Vernon Baker, a platoon leader in our regiment's First Battalion, led a combat patrol that captured a castle and wiped out a German force. He lost men but inflicted severe damage to the enemy. For his efforts, he was awarded the Distinguished Service Cross Medal while in Italy. That was the highest honor given to any soldier in the Ninety-Second Infantry Division during the war. The Medal of Honor, which he had been recommended to receive, was not given to him until 1997, fifty-two years after his outstanding combat action.

Finally, I must mention Lieutenant John M. Madison, the executive officer of Company I. By March 1, 1945, all the original officers of Company I, which had been led by Captain Jarman, except Madison had been killed in action. On April 4, leading his platoon in one of the final actions of the war, First Lieutenant John M. Madison was killed. Lieutenant Madison was posthumously awarded the Silver Star for his final heroic actions.

I am reciting battles, combat actions, and casualties because in an interview in November 1953, General Almond, the commanding officer of the Ninety-Second Infantry Division, said, among other things, "The white man is willing to die for patriotic reasons. The Negro is not." He also said, "We don't want to sit at the table with them." I'm certain he knew that several hundred black soldiers under his command had been killed in action, and many of them were cited for heroic action. As I said before, today over four hundred of my fellow Buffalo Soldiers are buried in the Florence American Cemetery and Memorial. Many others were returned to the States for burial. As I put in my first book, with God's help and the assistance of many other American fighting units, we were able to defeat Nazi Germany and Fascist Italy, but we did not conquer Jim Crow. I am certain General Almond's comments tainted the history of the Ninety-Second Infantry Division in a very negative way.

To the Italians, however, we were heroes. We gave them their liberty—and this leads me to the rest of the story, which started almost seventy years later.

CHAPTER 2

2012

In the spring of 2012, I received an email from my publisher, asking me if I would contact a woman in Italy, the owner of the villa my battalion captured in September 1944. This was of great interest to me, and by email I immediately contacted Mattea Piazzesi, the owner of the fifteenth-century Villa Orsini. Fortunately, Mattea speaks and writes English. The Villa Orsini is just five miles west of Lucca at Cerasomma, near where we crossed the Arno River and liberated the city of Lucca.

Mattea was updating the website of the villa which was renamed Villa La Dogana. Dogana means customs house which was the original use of the villa when the Orsini family owned it. The Orsini family built the villa and occupied it until around 1980 when Mattea's family purchased it and turned it into a bed and breakfast. Mattea wanted to use what I had written in my book about the capture of the villa on the villa's website. I was very happy to give her permission. Mattea emailed again and invited me to be a guest at the villa. I discussed this with my son and two daughters and found out that both of my daughters and their husbands could go with me. I am a widower, and I think they wanted to protect me! I told Mattea, who then extended the invitation to my entire family for a visit.

My family consists of my three adult children. I asked each of them to assist me by writing what they experienced. My daughter Pam is the oldest and is a retired paralegal. Pam is married to Paul Chretien, a retired civil engineer who ran his own business. Pam wrote,

> Growing up the in the fifties and sixties in Los Angeles, my siblings and I heard about World War II from our dad. Our beach blanket was his faded army green one. We grew up hearing place-names like Viareggio, Pisa, Massa, and Lucca. Faraway place-names wove in and out of our childhood. His wartime experiences had imprinted on our father when he was eighteen years old, and later they came to imprint on his children. In 2012, he told us he had been in email contact with an Italian woman in Lucca—Mattea Piazzesi, present owner of the Villa Orsini mentioned in the book.
>
> Before we left for Italy, I introduced myself to Mattea via email. The subject of the initial email read, "I am the daughter of the Buffalo Soldier." We chatted about motorcycles (we both have an interest in them) and Mexican food. I found out her family owns property in Mexico, where they visit often. I promised to make tacos when we got there. She promised to cook traditional Italian food for us. We put

together a press release and sent it to Mattea. She translated it and sent it out to the local and national Italian press. We were excited. She was excited.

My second daughter, Kathi, was born in 1951 in Los Angeles, California. Kathi is married to Dr. James Clyde Berryman Jr. They live near me in Los Angeles, and both decided to go on this trip to Italy. Kathi's older son, Barrett Johnson, is married to Jennifer Ramos, and they have two children, Sanaa and Brandon. Kathi's younger son is Jay Johnson, and he is married to Jeanne Roberts. They also have two children, Jay Jr. and Jeanne Kathleen. Their home is in St. Louis, Missouri. Kathi's daughter-in-law Jeanne's grandfather is also a World War II Buffalo Soldier who served in Italy. His name is Victor Roberts. He is ninety-five years young and living in St. Louis. As young soldiers, they traveled on the same ship to and from Italy during World War II but did not meet until their grandchildren began dating and the family pieced their stories together.

Kathi is retired from a program funded by the City of Los Angeles, Office of the Mayor, which provides gang prevention and intervention services. I have been a guest speaker at their programs and have distributed copies of my book about World War II to those attending. According to Kathi, the most asked question is, "What type of gun did you carry?" She was not surprised.

Kathi's husband, James, is a supervising senior pharmacist for the state of California. Both Kathi and James are active in the community, and both flew to Italy with me in 2012.

My daughter Kathi wrote,

> Growing up with Dad was always an adventure. The stories of his service in World War II remain with me to this day. My favorite was the story of Fortunato Sweeney, and it still delights me. According to Dad, his battalion was walking in the dangerous territory on a dark Italian night. Everyone had to be quiet and walk softly. The Buffalo Soldiers were in a single line, the path was narrow, and they could not see their hands in front of their faces. Each man put one hand on the shoulder of the man in front of him. As the long line silently snaked its way on the overgrown path, Sweeney let go of the shoulder of the man in front of him. Unfortunately, the man in front of Sweeney did not miss the slight pressure of Sweeney's hand behind him. Sweeney was now the leader of the men behind him, and he kept walking and walking and walking. He did not tell anyone behind him that he had let go of the man in front. No one realized what had happened, and Fortunato Sweeney lost the whole column and almost got everyone killed. As the sky began to get lighter, they were stopped from walking into a road intersection by their commanding colonel. He said the Germans were sweeping that intersection with machine-gun fire. They immediately sought shelter.
>
> As a child with a vivid imagination, I tried to imagine the anger and fear when they finally

realized they were lost and how it had happened. Years later, Sweeney sent his son Scott to work for our insurance company in Los Angeles. We shared this story with him and had a good laugh; after all, our dads survived to tell the story.

Dad talked a lot about Jody. "Jody" was the name soldiers gave to any guy who wasn't drafted. Jody was home with all the women. As they marched, they would chant, "Jody got your gal and gone. You had a good wife, but she left," and the response was, "You're right," chanting as they marched on the left or right foot. It was a great way to keep them marching in order.

Dad was wounded in WWII, and every year on the anniversary of being wounded, he feels pain in his shoulder where he was hit. Every year when we were kids, he would remind us, saying that his shoulder hurt. He would also drink grappa, the strong Italian liquor, from a special glass that came from the house where he had been wounded.

Best of all were the bedtime stories. Dad didn't read Mother Goose; he made up his own stories of the "Ant Armies," fighting under generals, winning battles, and falling back. He regaled us with ant military strategies. He brought so much of the war to our home we lived in at the time on Twenty-Fourth Street in Los Angeles.

When my parents moved to Ladera Heights in Los Angeles, they had a map with places Dad visited during the war. Later they both took trips to these areas. They came back amazed and delighted that partisans still remembered the Buffalo.

It was a very easy choice for James and me to travel with Dad, my sister, Pam, and my brother-in-law, Paul, to Italy in 2012. The war and its stories were always part of our lives, and we were as excited as Dad. Also, our mother had passed, and we were more than a little concerned about this mysterious Italian woman, who owned a villa, contacted Dad online, and invited him to her villa as her personal guest. This woman, Mattea, and her friends and family are now members of our family.

My youngest child is my son, Ivan Abbott Houston. He was born in Los Angeles in 1954. He has been married to Leslie Jackson-Houston, also a Los Angeles native, for over thirty years. Leslie retired from the entertainment industry as a television production manager and producer but recently was called back as a producer for a very popular television show. Ivan is also the godfather of his sister Kathi's son, Barrett, and he and Leslie are godparents of Barrett's daughter Sanaa.

Ivan's career started as an engineer in San Jose, California, working as a designer and test driver on military vehicles. Subsequently, he moved back to Los Angeles and worked as a computer engineer for the telephone company. After another career move, he became president of Golden State Minority

Foundation. The foundation supports college students and K–6 school programs.

In addition to his foundation duties, Ivan and his wife, Leslie, started a business called Ivan's Cooking LLC. The baking business specializes in artisan candies, cookies, and breads and has an international client base. Ivan is an exceptional baker and an excellent cook.

Ivan and I have had the pleasure of traveling together to some far-off places, starting with Italy in 2002. Ivan is also my technical support and graphic designer for my book, documentary, website, and other projects. Ivan has been to over thirty book signings with me and said, "Dad, since I've traveled with you to so many book signings, I find it amazing that people my age are fascinated by your story. Most of them have said that their fathers never talked about the war or that period of their lives. They all tend to agree that your book has enabled them to learn so much of the story they never heard but were affected by its impact growing up." He added, "I'm amazed at your recollection of so many events and am still learning from you."

Ivan was unable to come with us on our first visit to Lucca in 2012, but he has been by my side on every trip since. He sees the love I have for the region and seems to enjoy each visit.

In Italy, the information that one of the Buffalo Soldiers who helped liberate that part of Italy was coming for a visit began to make the rounds. An Italian army officer, Lieutenant Colonel Vittorio Biondi, a veteran of the Afghanistan war, took over my reception in Tuscany. I soon learned from Mattea that it looked like I was going to be very busy during my five-day stay at the villa. I told Mattea that was all right and that I would "go with the flow."

With my daughters and their husbands, I left Los Angeles on September 11, 2012. We flew to Rome and then to Pisa, where we were met by Mattea and her family. Mattea Piazzesi was just like the young Italian woman I met on a videoconference call when we were arranging our stay at the villa. She is animated and energetic and took charge of getting us oriented. She was with her young son, Lodovico, about ten years old; her husband, Marco Landucci; and her friend Marta Bertani. Marta lives in Lucca and helps Mattea manage the Villa La Dogana. Marco is a swimming coach. Only Mattea spoke English, but that didn't matter because our families became friendly at once. Communication was easy. They gave us hearty Italian hugs and kisses. It was a wonderful greeting, and we were off to the villa some twenty miles away.

Pam wrote about our arrival.

> We landed at the airport in Pisa on September 12, 2012. There to greet us were Mattea and her family. And flowers. My sister and I were each given a big bouquet of flowers. Our adventure was taking off beautifully. We drove in three cars to the villa, passing aqueducts and scenic countryside towns. At one point, we slowed down at a railroad crossing next to what I thought was another small village. To my surprise, we stopped and entered through gates. Dozens of people and children holding American flags were waving and greeting us. Men were dressed in vintage American army uniforms. Army surplus tents were set up. There were jeeps and motorcycles, and the Stars and Stripes was at full mast. We saw weapons and

ammo and period office equipment and first-aid supplies. We had arrived at the villa, and this fantastic sight greeted us. That's when it first dawned on me that this trip with Dad might be something other than a typical family vacation in a foreign country. What we were looking at were the Linea Gotica reenactors, who set up camp in the parkland that surrounded the villa. Chapters of this historical reenactment group are set up all over Italy.

The Tuscans, with their rich interwoven tapestry of history, have taken the Buffalo Soldiers to heart. They teach the history of their liberation from the Nazis in their schools and have monuments and plaques all over the place. And now, with Dad's arrival, they even have their very own Buffalo Soldier.

The Villa La Dogana is in Cerasomma, a suburb of Lucca. The villa was built in the fifteenth century by the Orsini family, an Italian noble family that was one of the most influential princely families in medieval Italy and Renaissance Rome. The Orsini family includes three popes: Pope Celestine III, Pope Nicholas III, and Pope Benedict XIII.

Lucca is a major city in Tuscany. Its population is about ninety thousand. The old part of the city is surrounded by a medieval wall that is beautiful to behold. The walls were initially built as defensive ramparts, and they were considered impressive military technology from the eleventh through the fifteenth centuries because they gave a full view from each rampart. But once they were not needed, they became pedestrian walkways. Lucca's history is very ancient. In 218 BCE, a Roman army, defeated by Hannibal of Carthage, retreated into Lucca. In 57 BCE, Julius Caesar, Pompey the Great, and Crassus, the most powerful men in the Roman Empire, met in Lucca to resolve their differences and divide up the empire. In the early 1800s, Elisa, a sister of Napoleon, ruled as princess of Lucca. It became part of Tuscany in the 1840s and finally part of the Italian state.

The grounds of the villa are very spacious, with wide, relaxing green lawns and shady seating areas to enjoy the country setting. World War II equipment in excellent condition was everywhere—jeeps, motorcycles, radios, typewriters, guns, and even food rations. Some of the soldiers were dressed in World War II German army uniforms and carried German weapons. Everyone greeted me, and frankly, I was in awe as I passed in review before a squad of soldiers dressed in American uniforms as they presented arms. They were excellent actors and knew how to handle the rifles and other equipment.

After the long trip from Los Angeles, about sixteen hours by air, we should have been exhausted, but we were all energized by the crowd. People wanted to shake my hand, give me a hug, and take my picture. I was happy to be with them.

The next morning, September 13, after breakfast in the villa dining area, with jams and strong coffee, to which we added hot foaming milk and sugar, we were off on an amazing tour, with Colonel Biondi, a lieutenant colonel in the Italian army, leading the group. Biondi, who lives in Lucca, learned that I was coming and organized my visit. He served with the Italian army in Afghanistan. I exchanged emails with him before the visit and described the battles I had been in and the places where we fought.

Our first stop was a beautiful old city building in Pietrasanta, which had been our headquarters from time to time in September and October 1944. The mayor of the city presented my daughters and me with gifts and flowers, and I gave the mayor a signed copy of my book. The ceremony was beautiful. The mayor, wearing a brilliantly colored Italian sash across his chest, stated what we would hear echoed again and again: "Thank you. Thank you. Thank you." A translator was provided for my family, and we listened as a spokesman told everyone what the Buffalo Soldiers had done for the Italians. He recounted my military history and my background as a successful African American businessman and touched on what had happened to the brave black soldiers when they returned to the United States. According to my daughter Kathi, our hostess, Mattea, asked, "What are Jim Crow laws?" The Italians were humbled that the black soldiers who had liberated them had returned to America as second-class citizens. This reality would resound repeatedly as we traveled from town to town.

Before we left Pietrasanta, we stopped at a beautiful white marble statue of Sadao Munemori holding his rifle, erected a few years earlier to memorialize the Japanese American soldier of the One Hundredth Battalion, 442nd Infantry Regiment. Munemori was killed in action on April 5, 1945, as our army assaulted the Gothic Line. For his heroic action, he was awarded the Medal of Honor. Munemori, like me, was from Los Angeles.

We left Pietrasanta in a caravan of jeeps and other vehicles and drove a few miles to the coast, where the Cinquale Canal empties into the Ligurian Sea. At that point a solid piece of white marble stands to mark the westernmost point of the famed Gothic Line. As I stated above, I was wounded on April 9, 1945. I was blown through the door of a large villa by enemy mortar fire just after crossing the canal at a place very near where the monument now stands. I was awarded the Purple Heart Medal for the wound that I received. A new monument to the Gothic Line, of a struggling man, woman, and child in white marble, has been erected on the highway that crosses the Cinquale Canal.

The Italians are very much preoccupied by the Gothic Line (Linea Gotica), the fortifications they built under German orders and that separated Fascist Italy, still run by Mussolini, from the Italy that had joined the Allied armies. If the Allied armies could break through the Gothic Line, the last line of defense in Italy, we would be getting very close to Southern Germany.

At noon on Thursday, September 13, our caravan drove to Viareggio, which is on the coast, a few miles south of the Cinquale Canal. In Viareggio we were hosted by the Principe di Piemonte Hotel. During the war, the hotel was the headquarters of the Ninety-Second Infantry Division. Hotel management honored me with a beautiful buffet, and I took pictures with the director. US World War II jeeps, with their squared-off front ends and canvas tops, were parked in front of the hotel. The green jeep was a World War II workhorse, used to transport troops, weapons, and wounded soldiers. They had special blackout headlights for convoys that could tilt up to illuminate the engine compartment.

I was paraded before a squad of reenactor soldiers dressed in World War II uniforms in front of the building where General Edward M. Almond, commanding general of the Ninety-Second Infantry Division, handed out decorations during the war. It was an amazing sight arranged by Colonel Biondi. An Italian crew filmed the memorable moment.

It was Colonel Biondi's idea to recreate the photo in my book *Black Warriors: The Buffalo Soldiers of World War II* that shows General Almond inspecting the troops of the Ninety-Second Division in front of the hotel. Traffic had to be stopped to get the jeeps, troops, and me in place in front of the five-star hotel. The citizens of Viareggio were wondering what was happening, and the people on the upper floors were looking out of their windows at the dramatic scene below. In the middle of all this appeared two women who had been in Italy during World War II. They never introduced themselves, but they recognized the American jeeps and uniforms; one had married an American soldier and proceeded to speak of the sad times and the good times all those years ago. Her husband was deceased. The other woman was in her nineties, in a wheelchair, accompanied by her caregiver. She too remembered those frightening days and expressed her thanks to me and all the Buffalo Soldiers who gave her and her compatriots their freedom.

The final event of the day was a buffet dinner and musical hosted by a wealthy American businessman, Bill Furman. Furman recently bought the Villa Salvi in the medieval city of Barga in the Apennine Mountains. My battalion first entered Barga in September 1944, and our headquarters was established there two months later. Barga was also the headquarters of a large Italian partisan group that fought with us and gave us valuable information about the enemy. Just to the north of Barga, atop a hill, stands the village of Sommacolonia, the site of Lieutenant John Fox's heroic stand. His valor in calling artillery on his own position on December 26, 1944, is still remembered in this community.

Furman spends a few days each year in Barga. He happened to be there during my visit, learned when I also would be there, and arranged a party. He followed my activities for the next two days, and I was happy to thank him with an autographed copy of my book.

On Friday morning, September 14, we returned to Barga. As we drove and later walked through the city, we saw posters along the way welcoming me, a returning Buffalo Soldier. The posters bore my picture and were in Italian and English. In the city council chambers of Barga, the mayor gave a speech praising the actions of the Buffalo Soldiers. Colonel Biondi introduced me and cited my military career, describing each medal I was wearing, and my activities in the civilian world after the war. I was given a beautiful etching of medieval Barga and many citations. With the help of an interpreter, I spoke briefly and gave autographed copies of my book to the mayor and another top official. In my speech, I said we had not seen much of Barga in daylight hours because during the war, we moved through the city after dark, not wanting to bring German guns down upon our positions. After the ceremony, we went out onto the balcony of the city hall and looked over the valley between Barga and Sommacolonia.

Sommacolonia was our next stop. We drove the short distance to that mountaintop village and then walked quite a distance up to the destroyed tower used by Lieutenant Fox as an observation point. We laid a wreath at the site, which I learned is now also dedicated to the victims of the 9/11 terrorist attack in the United States. It was truly amazing to learn that the tragedy of the war and the tragedy of that catastrophe are remembered together in this small Italian village. There were speeches by officials, and of course, I responded briefly.

My daughter Kathi wrote about Sommacolonia.

It is one of my favorite places, high up in the Italian mountains. The host wondered if Dad could make it up to the top. I knew he could, but I was worried about myself and my husband, James. The small village today only has about thirty residents. The ceremony was held in the remains of a castle that stood on the top of the mountain. This place is special because it is where Lieutenant John Fox met his death by calling his own artillery to fire on his position in order to stop the German offensive the day after Christmas in 1944. Apparently, many people thought Sommacolonia was a safe place during the war and sent their children there; they were so wrong. We climbed the steep path to the top of the mountain. There were several American and Italian flags that were blowing in the wind. The Alpini soldiers stood at attention with their green elf-like hats. They showed that they will forever bow to the bravery of the Buffalo Soldiers whom they fought against. (Italian Alpini soldiers fought with the Germans during the war.)

In this small community, on a steep cobblestone street, there is a wooden door with two artillery shells on either side. This is the entry to a museum dedicated to the soldiers of World War II. Inside, the residents have collected from the Italian mountains everything imaginable from the battles. This small museum has American,

Italian, and German weapons, uniforms, books, and ammunition. They also have photo albums of Lieutenant Fox and his family. My daughter said that they were very proud to add Dad's book to their collection. The residents cooked a lovely lunch with appetizers, pasta, and pork. The program included a talk by a resident who wrote a book on the war. She has become a close friend of Lieutenant Fox's widow and daughter.

We still had an important activity that night at the Villa La Dogana. My daughter Kathi, who was a guest at the dinner, shares her version of the dinner here.

Dad was knighted! He was made a member of the Sacro Militare Ordine Constantiniano di San Giorgio Delecazione Toscana (Sacred Military Order of Constantine of Giorgio Delegation of Tuscany). Our host, Mattea Piazzesi, had set a long formal table in the great hall of the villa. Battenburg lace tablecloths, fine china, sterling silver flatware, crystal glasses, and candles covered the tables. Dad sat at the head of the table, and the great hall had additional lighting. A formal five-course dinner was served by staff, starting with a Tuscan bean soup, then two kinds of pasta, thin-sliced pork roast with roasted potatoes, and gelato for dessert. It reminded me of every classic Italian movie. After dinner, Colonel Biondi presented Dad with a gorgeous framed gold medal set in a plaque. What a lovely, lovely time we had that night.

It was a great honor for me.

On Saturday morning, September 15, we were taken to Bagni di Lucca, another city liberated by my regiment. On the way we stopped at a roadside gathering of another organization involved with the Gothic Line Association and had coffee and cake. I shook hands with many people who were happy to see this Buffalo Soldier. When we reached Bagni di Lucca, we were greeted by the mayor and taken to the city hall, where speeches and gifts were exchanged. My gift to the mayor was an autographed copy of my book. I was given a very large box that contained a hand-carved nativity set, which is a specialty of this town. The beautiful set arrived at my home in Los Angeles just before Christmas. I set it up each year and remember the wonderful people of Bagni di Lucca. After our meeting in the city hall, the mayor, his officials, my "soldier" escorts, and I walked through the town, greeted by crowds of people. American and Italian flags were everywhere.

From the city hall in Bagni di Lucca, we were taken to the city's most famous bathhouse for another presentation and ceremony. The white stucco bathhouse is built into a verdant mountain that contains hot springs. Here I was given a white bathrobe in my size, and we were all served coffee and lunch. Bagni di Lucca is famous not only for its nativity sets but also for its natural thermal baths. Our final stop in the city was the English graveyard. The sister of American president Grover Cleveland is buried there. She died in 1918 in Bagni di Lucca, trying to help people during the great flu epidemic.

That evening, Mattea Piazzesi and her husband, Marco Landucci, hosted a grand party on the grounds of the Villa La Dogana. World War II army tents and equipment were everywhere on display. There was much music and dancing.

All the reenactors whom I had seen since my arrival at the villa were present. There were nurses, WACS, and soldiers dressed in World War II American uniforms. Others were dressed in German and Alpini (Italian Alpine troops) uniforms. It was a grand occasion. Colonel Biondi's wife and three children were present, along with the children of the other participants in my welcome and processions through many towns and villages. I retired about eleven o'clock, but the music and dancing went on.

On Sunday, September 16, Mattea and Marco, together with their son Lodovico and friend Marta, drove my family in their two cars about fifty miles to the Florence American Cemetery and Memorial. The cemetery is in Falciani, Italy, and is built on the rolling hills of Tuscany. Each grave site has a white marble cross or Star of David, the name of the soldier, his date of death, his unit, and the state he was from. This is the cemetery for 4,398 members of the US armed forces killed in the battles of Northern Italy. There is a memorial wall listing 1,409 persons missing in action. As near as can be determined and including the separate 366th Infantry Regiment, there are some four hundred African American Buffalo Soldiers buried in that cemetery. It is a very beautiful yet solemn sight.

The superintendent of the cemetery is a retired US Army sergeant, John Luncheon, an African American. My son, Ivan A. Houston, and I met him in 2002 when we visited the cemetery with a group from the Catholic Archdiocese of Los Angeles. Sunday is his day off, but when he heard of my visit, he had to be there. He showed us the graves of James E. Reed, Barry Seixus, Jesse Jarman, Hugh Portee, George Gray, and Lester Lightfoot, all men I had known and mentioned in my book. The great memorial wall of the cemetery, done in marble and mosaic tile, shows the battles and campaigns that took place in Northern Italy during World War II. The actions of the Ninety-Second Infantry Division are shown in arrows imbedded with the buffalo insignia. In no other place in the world are Buffalo Soldiers memorialized as they are in this cemetery. I autographed a book for John Luncheon. People who visit the cemetery ask him many questions about the soldiers buried there, and he had been asked about the first Buffalo Soldier killed in Italy. Now he has the answer: Staff Sergeant James E. Reed, Company I, 370th Infantry Regiment was the first black infantry soldier killed in Europe, on August 24, 1944. It has always been my contention that the Florence American Cemetery and Memorial has more African American infantry combat soldiers than any other cemetery in the world.

My final excursion of this trip took place Sunday afternoon at the small community of Aquileia and the city of Borgo a Mozzano. We drove to Aquileia in World War II army vehicles and once again were given a wonderful greeting. We were served coffee and cake and took many pictures. Newspaper articles showing my visit were spread out on tables for all to see. Apparently, the fact I was there was of great interest to the people of this region. After visiting Aquileia, we went to Borgo a Mozzano, a city where there are still remnants of the fortified Gothic Line. Even though it was Sunday, we met in city council chambers, and the assistant mayor spoke and gave me a plaque commemorating my visit from one of the Gothic Line organizations.

My daughter Kathi and her husband, James, and I left the Villa La Dogana on September 17. We returned to Los Angeles after spending three days in Rome. My other daughter, Pam, and her husband, Paul, remained at the villa for another week.

While at the villa, I had been given a letter by one of the reenactors, Flavio. I was so busy that I did not open it until I was home and unpacking the wonderful gifts that had been given to me. I thought about my visit to the villa and those towns and villages in Tuscany. The gratitude of the people greeting me was almost overwhelming. I wondered why. Then I opened and read Flavio's letter. It is translated as written.

To Mr. Ivan J. Houston

"With immense pleasure"

Mr. Ivan, I felt to write a few lines to prove the immense love and eternal gratitude that I have toward the American people and especially the Buffalo Soldiers.

I am forty-five, and I have not experienced the tragedies and horrors of the greatest tragedy of humanity.

If, however, I am a free man and many others like me, I can only thank you US soldiers. We have been freed from our oppressor by the sacrifice of so many guys fighting on every front, from the Atlantic to the Pacific, on the sea, in the air, and on the ground.

My father since I was a child always told me that you "Mori" (Editor's note: the name used to describe black warriors coming from Africa since the Middle Ages) offered him the first chocolate a long time ago in September 1944. In my mind I've always thought of you as the "good Giants"; in fact, you are my heroes.

By profession I'm a trader; in my spare time I'm a reenactor. Look at the case of the GI soldier, especially the First Infantry Division Big Red One. When I act as a GI, I can feel it on my skin, because I know in the deep of my heart that someone (you) came to save us from a long distance. So it is with "immense pleasure" that I write you, and in my life I'll be able to tell of having met one of the "good giants," my heroes.

I wish you my best greetings of welcome wishing you a great stay, saying thank you from the deep of my heart.

Flavio

This letter explained my wonderful reception and the celebrations, and it moved me to know that what we did was important. When I later learned that the city of Lucca, which we liberated on September 5, 1944, annually celebrates that liberation, I was determined to go back and participate in the celebration.

The Villa La Dogana

Arrival at the villa

Becoming a knight at the grand banquet

Discussing the grand banquet with Mattea at the villa

Grand banquet at Villa when I was knighted

Grave site of first WWII Buffalo Soldier killed in
combat with Superintendent John Luncheon

Grave site of heroic Captain Jesse Jarman

Honoring Sadao Munemori at Pietrasanta

In Viareggio reviewing WWII reenactors

Meeting with city officials in Barga

Meeting with city officials in Pietrasanta

Memorial to Lieutenant John Fox in Sommacolonia

The mountaintop village of Sommacolonia

My entrance into the Villa La Dogana

New Gothic Line monument in Cinquale Canal

Parading in the streets of Bagni di Lucca

Receiving the nativity set in Bagni di Lucca

Small museum in Sommacolonia

Welcome poster in Barga

With my family at Old Gothic Line monument

With Mattea Piazzesi

CHAPTER 3

2013

After returning from Italy in 2012, I discussed the wonderful reception I had been given by the Italians in Tuscany and my visit to places the Buffalo Soldiers had fought and the Florence American Cemetery and Memorial, where many of our dead are buried. My friend Gordon Cohn, who helped me write my book *Black Warriors: The Buffalo Soldiers of World War II*, was one of those who thought a documentary film should be made so that many others could see and appreciate the contribution the Buffalo Soldiers had made in liberating Italy. We decided the title of the documentary film would be *The Good Giants*, a phrase also used in Flavio's letter, which was reproduced in the previous chapter.

After my visit in 2012, I learned that the city of Lucca celebrated its liberation by the Buffalo Soldiers of my regiment, the 370th, each year in September. In 2012, I missed this celebration. I had already planned to go to Italy to celebrate this, so we decided to film parts of the documentary at the same time.

I left Los Angeles on an Alitalia flight to Rome on the afternoon of September 5, 2013. My daughter Pam; her husband, Paul; and my son, Ivan, were with me for this visit as guests at the Villa La Dogana.

We arrived in Rome the next day and, after a layover, flew from Rome to Pisa. While in the Rome airport, we met Dennis McCoy, father of Dan McCoy, the sound producer on the documentary we had begun to film on events that occurred following my return to Italy after publication of *Black Warriors: The Buffalo Soldiers of World War II*. All of us, including Dennis, a photographer, headed to the villa.

We arrived at the Pisa International Airport in less than an hour and were met by Mattea Piazzesi; her husband, Marco Landucci; son, Lodovico; and a great friend, Marta Bertani. Pam and Paul rented a blue Fiat at the airport, and we were soon off to the villa. On the way, Mattea drove us through Ripafratta, a small village near the villa that had been the site of a vicious battle in which my regiment was engaged after we crossed the Arno River on September 1, 1944. That day in 2013, it was all very peaceful and tranquil. There was no way to tell that sixty-nine years earlier, tanks rumbled through the streets, while the infantry and artillery echoed off the cobblestones. We soon arrived at the villa, and I was given the same room I had occupied in 2012. My room was the Magnolia Room, and a very realistic artificial magnolia was hung on the door. The room was very large, with a king-size bed and other furniture. There was a separate bathroom off the entry hallway.

Outside the villa, on spacious grounds, World War II reenactors had set up camp. Vehicles, World War II jeeps and tanks, tents, guns, and people were everywhere. Reenactors try to have equipment and clothing relevant to the period, and they help keep history alive. The villa is quite large, three stories; only the first two stories, however, were being used as a bed-and-breakfast. The grounds of the villa cover a few acres, and there is much foliage, including a very large magnolia tree.

On Saturday, September 7, the other members of the documentary team—director, producer, soundman Dan McCoy, and the camera crew of Guido Frenzel and Rod Hassler—joined us. Other members of the production and film crew soon followed. The team's assignment was to follow me around and capture the events of my visit. Later, we were to be joined by Sarah Craddock Morrison, US Counsel General residing in Florence, and members of her staff. Counsel General Morrison had been contacted by her good friend and one of the associate producers of the documentary, Giulia Scarpa. Giulia is a professor at the University of Bologna and an outstanding translator (English, French, and Italian), who would also be traveling with me during my stay and seemingly effortlessly translate my ramblings and the wordy monologues of Italian officials, who always had something interesting to say. When Giulia was not present, Mattea would step in as a translator. It was great working with these wonderful women.

I visited the encampments of the reenactors on the large grounds of the villa with Counsel General Morrison. The encampment was even larger than last year when I paid my first visit. The World War II jeeps were in excellent condition, and I had to sign several of them on their hoods. I also signed World War II helmets and even pieces of camouflage. The fact I had been present during the fighting that liberated the villa sixty-nine years ago was not lost on those there. Some of the reenactors were dressed as German soldiers, carried German arms, and even lived on the villa grounds in German field tents. Other reenactors were dressed like those Italians who fought for the Fascists, and some wore the peaked hats like those of the Alpini soldiers, who also fought for the Fascists. Here they were all together having a great time, and all wanted their picture taken with me. Counsel General Morrison talked to each group and enjoyed the visit. That evening ended with a big party featuring a band that played 1940s music and dancing on the patio of the villa.

Sunday, September 8, was the day I had been waiting for. This year I would be in the lead jeep with Italian reenactors dressed as World War II American soldiers as we entered the city. Mattea was in my jeep, dressed in the uniform of a Buffalo Soldier captain. Ousmane, an African Italian reenactor, was also in my jeep manning a mounted machine gun. What an honor! During World War II, Lucca was liberated by the Second Battalion of Combat Team 370 on the morning of September 5, 1944. Captain Charles Gandy of Company F had led his force of Buffalo Soldiers through the gates of this ancient walled city.

The next day, while in the city of Lucca, I was given the book *History of Lucca* by British historian and World War II artilleryman John Jones. His book describes Lucca when Hannibal of Carthage crossed the Alps with his elephants around 218 BCE. Hannibal's forces defeated a Roman army, which retreated into Lucca. The book describes the meeting at Lucca in 57 BCE between Julius Caesar, Pompey the Great, and Crassus to divide the Roman Empire. Jones also writes about Napoleon's beloved sister Elisa, who ruled the city during the early 1800s. His book ends with the stirring account of the final liberation of Lucca by my regiment of Buffalo Soldiers.

The 370th Infantry Regiment crossed the Arno River on September 1. Our main goal was capturing the city of Lucca. By the evening of September 2, our troops, along with tanks and engineers, and battling the 65th German Grenadiers, succeeded in taking Mount Pisano, the commanding feature of the area. We moved through the villages and towns of Lugnano, Uliveto, Caprona, and Asciano, all on the north side of the river, east of Pisa. Captain Jarman, Company I, and Captain Brown, Company L, moved quickly toward San Giuliano to establish a defense perimeter around its edges. Our mission, however, suddenly changed. It was decided that we would attack rather than defend. Companies I and L moved out, with light and medium tanks at the head of each company. We were intent on getting to Lucca.

As our attack moved ahead, our battalion was hit by tremendous artillery barrages—more than five hundred rounds. Regimental headquarters ordered the Third Battalion to capture the fifteenth-century Villa Orsini (now the Villa La Dogana) and the village of Ceresomma. Both of these objectives, en route to Lucca, were secured on September 4.

On September 5, 1944, Lucca was liberated. Company F, commanded by Captain Charles Gandy, entered the city, and a regimental command post was established in one of the city's hotels.

I only recently found out what happened to the residents inside the city of Lucca as fighting raged outside its walls.

Dr. Janna Merrick, professor, School of Interdisciplinary Global Studies at the University of South Florida, visits Lucca every year. After reading *Black Warriors: The Buffalo Soldiers of World War II,* she shared the following story with me: She met an older Italian lady who had been a young woman in 1944, when we were fighting to capture Lucca from the Germans. Her name was Liliana, and she had hidden inside the wall— hungry, tired, and, of course frightened. She fell asleep but awoke to find a young black soldier from our unit, tugging at her arm. Through an interpreter, the soldier said, "You are safe now. The Americans are here. We have food for you." And with that, he led her out from her hiding place inside the wall and into a liberated Lucca!

Dr. Merrick visited Lucca in 2017. This time, she carried a letter and photos from me to Liliana and videoed the highlights of that visit. Dr. Merrick wrote that even at ninety-six years-old, Liliana remembered the liberation as though it happened yesterday. She said that the day after the Buffalo Soldiers liberated Lucca, she and other townspeople danced in the streets with the soldiers from our unit. In Dr. Merrick's video, tears fell from Liliana's eyes because she was so grateful that the soldiers from my unit and I had saved her life and the lives of her friends and family members. Liliana also understood that in saving her life, many American soldiers lost their own lives. As the Italians have said, "The Americans gave us the sweetest fruit of the tree; they gave us our lives and our freedom, but we know it wasn't free. The Americans gave us our lives with their blood and the loss of their own lives."

As a soldier with the 370th Infantry, I did not enter the walled city of Lucca. After liberating the Villa Orsini and the village of Cerasomma, my battalion, the Third, reached the western gate of the city, and I remember marveling at those amazing walls. Now, sixty-nine years later, I rode with the reenactors as we entered Lucca from Porta San Pietro (Saint Peter's Gate). We were greeted by many people on the narrow streets as we made our way to the *Cortile degli Svizzeri* (Swiss Courtyard). It is not a square because it is inside the *Palazzo Ducale* (Ducal Palace) and was named so because the soldiers paid by the Republica di Lucca in the seventeenth century had their barracks on the southern side of the *cortile* (courtyard).

The mercenaries were *Guardie Svizzere* (Swiss Guards, who guarded the pope).

After we entered Lucca, the reenactors' vehicles parked in the Piazza Napoleone courtyard. A large number of residents and tourists came to see the vehicles and the reenactors and to talk to me. Everybody had a story about World War II. Stories had apparently been passed down from grandparents and parents. I had a wonderful time and signed vehicles and all kinds of articles of clothing. I was quite honored just seeing the crowds and was amazed that they were still celebrating the liberation of Lucca by Buffalo Soldiers and had reenacted this liberation. There was no reenactment of the fighting because when we liberated Lucca, the Germans were gone. The fighting took place outside the walls of the city of Lucca.

When we left the courtyard, all of us, including the reenactors, went to lunch at the Angeli Bar Ristorante Pizzeria, a restaurant outside the walls of Lucca. It was an excellent meal, and the pasta was great!

On September 9, we returned to the Palazzo Ducale for a program with the provincial president of Lucca and other officials. We were in a great room with a high ceiling and beautiful paintings on the walls. The room overlooked one of the important piazzas of the city, and from one of the windows, Mattea showed us the bar that she and her husband, Marco, owned before they moved to the villa. John Luncheon, the superintendent of the Florence American Cemetery and Memorial, was present. Lucca officials presented me with books, plaques, and medals. One medal, struck with the seal of Lucca and celebrating the 150th anniversary of the unification of Italy, had been presented to only four other individuals.

In the early months of 2013, Mattea Piazzesi had begun translating my book *Black Warriors: The Buffalo Soldiers of World War II* into Italian. I worked with her, and we made great progress. Later, Mattea contacted Francesca Fazzi, owner of the book publisher Maria Pacini Fazzi of Lucca. Fazzi made a decision to publish my book in Italian and used Giulia Larturo from the language department of the University of Pisa for the translations. I first met Francesca Fazzi and Giulia Larturo at the program in the Palazzo Ducale on September 9. We discussed the translation of my book from English to Italian.

Later, on September 9, at the Villa La Dogana, I met the son and widow of the artist Bruno Tintori, Roberto Tintori and his mother, Irma. My wife, Philippa, and I had met Bruno Tintori while we were walking along the beachfront during our visit to Viareggio in 1978. He recognized me as a Buffalo Soldier when I told him in Italian that I was here in Viareggio in 1944 and 1945. He started hugging me and kissing me. He then told me he was one of the partisans who helped us carry ammunition into the mountains. It was a very emotional meeting, and we went next door to a bar and had a few glasses of grappa, a uniquely Italian drink. I mentioned him in the concluding pages of my book *Black Warriors: The Buffalo Soldiers of World War II.*

The Tintori family gave me a landscape painting by the late artist and partisan. They were very happy that I had mentioned him. Bruno Tintori was an unforgettable character because many Italian movie stars were his clients, and he was referred to as "the artist to the stars." The widow of Tintori did not want to be interviewed, but once she started talking, it seemed that she would never stop—a wonderful lady.

Our final visitors at the villa on September 9 were two members of the Orsini family. The Villa La Dogana was called the Villa Orsini when we captured it in September 1944. Now we were visiting with two surviving members of the family that had built the villa in the fifteenth century. The young woman, Alessandra Orsini, and her uncle Paolo Orsini were very nice. Members of our documentary team interviewed them. The father of Alessandra Orsini was living at the villa when the Buffalo Soldiers of my battalion arrived during World War II. Apparently, the villa had been some type of headquarters for the German army before we captured it.

On Tuesday, September 10, the film crew began filming me as I walked along the Serchio River, which runs behind the Villa La Dogana. My daughter and son, Pam and Ivan A., and I were to stroll along the riverbank and discuss how it might have been when my regiment crossed and sometimes had to cross that river several times. As I remember, in September 1944, the river was quite high from recent rains, and one of the Buffalo Soldiers drowned during the crossing. My daughter did not want to discuss the fact I was frequently being shot at by all sorts of weapons as we fought along the Serchio River. A railroad track was nearby where we strolled, and from time to time a train would pass. The sound of the train reminded me that my father, an artillery officer in the Ninety-Second Infantry Division during World War I, told me that the artillery shells flying overhead would have the sound of a freight train, and they did.

That afternoon we drove south over the Arno River, attempting to find the Villa Remaggi, a sprawling farm complex that was the command post of my battalion when we entered combat on the night of August 23, 1944. I looked in vain for the tower that had been an outpost staffed by the scout observers of the Third Battalion. Many changes had taken place since 1944, and I was not able to identify the Villa Remaggi. The Germans bombed one of our outposts near the Villa Remaggi at night just after we entered combat, wounding several of our soldiers. I remember going out at night and walking through grape fields that were heavy with ripe grapes. We went out at night to avoid being seen and shot at by the Germans.

We crossed the Arno River again and walked along the north side, trying to determine just where my battalion had crossed in 1944. The bridge we drove across is on the same site where army engineers had built a Bailey bridge for vehicles to cross in 1944. A photo in a nearby restaurant showed the old bridge with army vehicles crossing in 1944. The Arno riverbanks do not look today like they did in 1944. In 1944 there was no growth along the river, but now the banks are covered with much green foliage. We returned to the Villa La Dogana, once again passing through Ripafratta, the small village that was the site of fierce fighting as our regiment and the tanks of the First Armored Division fought our way toward Lucca.

On Wednesday, September 11, we drove as close as possible to Hills X, Y, and Z. These hills look today pretty much like they looked during our fierce battles in 1944 and 1945. Many black officers and enlisted men were killed or wounded fighting for those hills. During the fighting, very little vegetation covered X, Y, and Z. Now, a lot of nondescript vegetation can be seen. Now they are peaceful; during the war. just being seen in the near vicinity would bring much enemy firepower down on any soldier. Capturing those nameless hills resulted in hundreds of casualties. They were the site of many battles and were close to the village of Strettoia, frequently the target of artillery fire.

We drove on to the city of Seravezza and Mount Cauala, where we had suffered our worst casualties. I saw the place where I tried to get ammunition from Seravezza to the top of Mount Cauala. The route to the top of the mountain looks the same as it did almost seventy years ago. Those of us with that ammunition detail were blasted by artillery and machine-gun fire. We did not make it to the top of the mountain. It is a steep climb, and I see why some of our soldiers had to use rope ladders as they worked their way to the top.

Just remembering what it was like almost seventy years ago with machine-gun fire raking our position and artillery shells exploding all around is still a problem for me. I don't have nightmares, but when I think or talk about that experience, my hands sometimes tremble so much that I am unable to write my own name.

After the battle at Seravezza, my battalion was pulled out of line, and we walked back to the city of Pietrasanta. On the way to Pietrasanta, we stopped in a peaceful meadow at a place called L'Argentiera. It seemed to be the only level piece of ground in the mountainous city of Seravezza. As our documentary team drove along, I continually looked for L'Argentiera but without success.

Finally, we came to the Palazzo Mediceo, dedicated to the citizens of Seravezza for their bravery during the war. The palazzo is a large two-story building with a number of meeting rooms. It is white, with open balconies that look out on the mountains surrounding that community. At the Palazzo Mediceo, we enjoyed a wonderful program in which I was presented honors by the mayor and some of the citizens. Frankly, I was deeply touched by the people who came to thank me for what the Buffalo Soldiers had done for them during the war—giving them their freedom. I met one of the partisans who fought with us in this region. He and I were the same age, eighty-eight. Some sixty-nine years after the battle of Seravezza and Mount Cauala, I talked to the father of Ettore Neri, the mayor of Seravezza. He was a boy of twelve years during the war. He said that for days after the battle, he and other young Italians were carrying bodies of Buffalo Soldiers down from Mount Cauala for burial. They were doing the job so fast that the Americans told them, "Take it easy!" They now commonly use the slang *takiteasy*, which means "slow down."

We had lunch in Seravezza as guests of the mayors of Seravezza and Stazzema. After lunch, the mayor of Stazzema took us to that village, which was the site of a massacre of 560 local villagers, including 130 children, on August 12, 1944. This crime was committed by the Nazis and the Fascists while my regiment of Buffalo Soldiers was in Italy but had not yet reached the front line at the Arno River. The massacre was at the church of Saint Anna and was the subject of director Spike Lee's film *Miracle at St. Anna*. Today, the simple sixteenth-century church has been rebuilt and is across from a World War I monument and a wonderful museum. The museum includes photos of World War II Buffalo Soldiers fighting to liberate that part of Italy.

On Thursday, September 12, I went with the documentary team and Solace Wales, an American writer who has a home in Sommacolonia and is an expert on the 366th Infantry Regiment, to the Gothic Line monument at the Cinquale Canal. Solace and I walked up and down the beach and talked about the puzzle of the 366th, the regiment commanded by black officers. They suffered heavy casualties at Sommacolonia in the December 26 German counteroffensive and additional heavy casualties in the February 8–10 attack on the Cinquale

Canal and Hills X, Y, and Z. These casualties were never officially accounted for. The 366th was disbanded, and its surviving soldiers became service troops—no longer combat soldiers because there were no combat-trained black infantry soldiers available as replacements. White soldiers who were not officers could not be sent to the 366th or any regiment of the Ninety-Second Infantry Division because they would be commanded by black officers and noncommissioned officers, and that was against army policy. It was certainly brilliant planning—not! Amazingly, there are no official records of any casualties suffered by the 366th Infantry Regiment, yet more than one hundred soldiers of this regiment are buried at the Florence American Cemetery and Memorial. Many others were sent home for burial after the war.

An Italian named Alberti, who was a teenager during the war, was present at the Cinquale Canal monument and invited the documentary team and the reenactors to a luncheon at his home in Massa. Mr. Alberti has an amazing World War II museum in his home—German, Italian, British, and American battlefield equipment, all in excellent condition. While at the luncheon, Fred Kuwornu, an Italian African film director, caught up with us. Fred produced the documentary film *Inside Buffalo*, about the Ninety-Second Division.

I first met Fred in Los Angeles in 2010 after my book had been published. Fred was visiting and showing his documentary to audiences in Los Angeles and San Francisco. In Los Angeles, Fred showed his film *Inside Buffalo*, and I had a book signing for *Black Warriors: The Buffalo Soldiers of World War II* at the African American Museum, the University of Southern California, and the Mamie Clayton Library and Museum. We repeated the joint presentation at the Golden Gate Club of the Presidio of San Francisco for a program sponsored by the Italian Cultural

Institute. Fred and I arranged to meet in New York when I was invited to be a guest on a BET program regarding post-traumatic stress disorder. Fred was living in New York at that time.

On the evening of Friday, September 13, our friend Marta Bertani, a resident of the city of Lucca, took us to a building with a balcony where we could view the procession for the Festival of Santa Croce (the Holy Cross). Prior to the procession, we went into the Duomo of Lucca, the Cathedral of San Martino. The cathedral was rebuilt in the Gothic style in the fourteenth century and has impressive, tall columns and a bell tower. I entered the right-hand nave, which is only open for two festivals, May 3 and September 13. There in the octagonal chapel, I saw *Il Volto Santo* (the Holy Face of Lucca, or Sacred Countenance). It is a larger-than-life-size statue of Jesus Christ on the cross. The statue is eight feet by nine feet, but that's not what struck me the most. I noticed the face of Jesus, and it was very dark, almost black, and this made a lasting impression on me. The crucifix shows Christ alive and triumphant over death on the cross. Christ is untroubled by pain or suffering. I had never seen anything like it, and I felt compelled to learn more about it.

Looking back almost seventy years, I felt it was remarkable that black soldiers from my regiment liberated the ancient walled city of Lucca during the worst war in the history of civilization, and a crucifix of a black Jesus Christ was in the cathedral of that city and had been there for over a thousand years. I don't think anyone in our regimental combat team was aware of this when we liberated the city in 1944.

We left the cathedral on the evening of September 13, following the traditional procession of Il Volto Santo. The procession is called the Luminaria. At night, Lucca is illuminated by thousands of candles in a way that makes the entire center of the city glow. Those marching in the procession were from the church parishes, church organizations, and community organizations in the region of Lucca. A large image of Il Volto Santo is carried in the procession. From the balcony, we had a wonderful view. We went down from our balcony and mingled with the crowd. Many were carrying candles. What an inspiring evening!

One of the reenactors, dressed in a Buffalo Soldier uniform, was an African from Guinea-Bissau, a small sub-Saharan country in Northwest Africa. His name is Ousmane Dosso. He has two African preteen children, but he is married to an Italian woman. They are a lovely family. On September 14, Ousmane and I were filmed walking on top of the famous walls of Lucca. We talked about his life in Italy, and I learned that he has three jobs. He is a driver for a hospital, a house painter, and a gardener. Ousmane said he works a lot because that is the only way to get ahead. As we walked along the very broad road atop the walls, he pointed out where he and his wife were married and where they had their reception. I learned that Ousmane became a reenactor because his grandfather fought for the French in Paris during World War II. (His grandfather was with the French Colonial troops fighting with US soldiers when Paris was liberated from the Germans in 1944.) Giulia Scarpa was translating for Ousmane and me as we walked the walls, and from time to time, he would start talking in French. This change in language did not cause problems for Giulia since she is also fluent in that language. Ousmane says he is sometimes slighted by Italians, but they accept him because he is a hard worker.

We did not discuss how Ousmane was slighted, but black people in a predominately white society often have difficulties being accepted. I was always told that I would have to be twice as good at what I was doing if I wanted to be successful in this society. This unwritten challenge probably helped me throughout my life. I am certain Ousmane feels he must work twice as hard as a native Italian in order to become successful. We finished our walk and talk along the wall of Lucca at a gelato shop and had delicious ice cream.

It rained on Sunday, September 15, and we relaxed at the villa. That afternoon we had a visit from an Italian woman about my age. Her name was Silvana Galli. She became pregnant by a Buffalo Soldier during the war. She had written a book, the translated title of which is *Little Blonde*. With Giulia translating, Silvana described her affair with the Buffalo Soldier, the birth of her son, and her life in general. Present during this entire interview were her son and his daughter. Her son looked like a dark-skinned Italian, but her granddaughter was blonde and white. Silvana said their life had been very interesting with its ups and downs. The granddaughter spoke from time to time, but during the whole interview, the son was very silent. According to Silvana, other girls had done the same things that she did, but she just happened to become pregnant. She now owns a beachfront house and invited me and my family to be her guests.

There were several thousand young African American Buffalo Soldiers and many young Italian women in the cities and towns we liberated. Many of the younger Italian men were away fighting the war. Some relationships did develop between some of the women and the soldiers. Silvana's story is how one of those relationships happened.

When I became battalion sergeant major after the war ended, I remember a young Buffalo Soldier who got a young Italian girl pregnant and wanted to take her home with him. They came into battalion headquarters, and I could see they wanted to be together. We had no procedures to handle these kinds of situations. The soldier was sent home to the United States, and I don't know what happened to the young girl. Looking back, I hope they stayed in contact and somehow got together.

On Monday, September 16, we drove to the Apennine mountain village of Abetone. During the war, combat patrols from our battalion reached this point briefly as we fought our way up Highway 12, a very mountainous road. The Germans blew up most of the highway, and much of it had fallen into the Terme Lima—a small river that flows along the highway. Today the river flows peacefully, with no sign of the conflict that happened during the war.

Mattea Piazzesi's family has a restaurant in Abetone, and we stopped there for lunch. Abetone is a ski resort, and a ski run is directly in front of the restaurant. With the musicians playing, Giulia Scarpa, our illustrious translator, and I danced. For a while during the war, Abetone was the headquarters of German Field Marshal Albert Kesselring. His headquarters was in the woods across from the restaurant. We learned that Abetone was occupied by the Germans in 1943 when the Italian government ousted Mussolini and surrendered. The Italians living in Abetone were given just a few minutes to pack up and leave. I learned much about Abetone as Mattea and I were filmed talking and walking through the woods. Being in this setting gave everyone present some idea of the type of terrain we faced as we attacked the Gothic Line.

On Tuesday, we went to the Florence American Cemetery and Memorial. I visited the graves of some of the soldiers I had known, and we filmed footage for the documentary. At the cemetery's memorial building, the buffalo patch, the insignia of the Ninety-Second Infantry Division, in black and gold mosaic tile, is shown with the insignias of the other units that fought in the battles of northern Italy. The insignias are shown together with the very large mural that is a part of the cemetery memorial. This huge mural shows the battles that took place in Northern Italy. Along the Ligurian (western) coast, an arrow in the mural shows the Buffalo Soldiers of the Ninety-Second Infantry Division advancing toward the city of Genoa.

On Wednesday, September 18, we drove to Ripafratta to film the scene of one of our early battles—September 4, 1944. The terrain is flat, and that was the reason the infantry used tanks in the attack. As discussed in this book, Major Biggs, regimental executive officer, and several other soldiers were killed or wounded in that battle. During combat, I tried to stay away from tanks. Their dust and noise brought lots of artillery fire down on their position. An infantry soldier was unprotected if caught in that deluge of fire.

Also on the eighteenth, I was interviewed for the documentary on the third floor of the Villa La Dogana in a room that hadn't been used for more than one hundred years. I was trying to think about Mattea's invitation to visit in 2012, about the warm welcome given me and my family by the people of Tuscany, about Flavio's letter that finally turned a light on in my head about the meaning of the visit, and about this recent visit and how grateful the Italians continue to feel toward the Buffalo Soldiers who fought to give them their freedom. During this interview, I said, "This is the first time in history that African American soldiers liberated another people." By this I meant the several cities, towns, and villages in the region of Tuscany where we fought and especially the city of Lucca.

We left the villa the next day for our flight home to Los Angeles. The year 2014 would be the seventieth anniversary of the liberation of Lucca, and I was already planning to return for that celebration.

African Italian reenactor Ousmane, his daughter, and his wife

Autographing a helmet with Counsel General Morrison

Versilia, una jeep americana con alcuni soldati della "Buffalo".
In primo piano il capitano Charles F.Jr Gandy, comandante
della prima pattuglia entrata a Lucca.
Cadrà il 12 ottobre 1944 durante i combattimenti sul monte

Buffalo Soldiers entering Lucca September 5, 1944

Entering the walls of Lucca in 2013

Family, friends, and reenactors at the villa

Filming with Giulia Scarpa in Seravezza

Florence cemetery with Superintendent John Luncheon

Giulia Larturo, translator, and Francesca Fazzi, publisher

Hills X, Y, and Z—gentle slopes where many died

In Seravezza with Ettore Neri, mayor of Seravezza
and Riccardo Biagi, city council president

In Seravezza, a World War II battlefield with Ivan A.

L'Argentiera, valley where we rested after Seravezza battle

Lucca officials and reenactors

Presented honors in Lucca

Reenactor Flavio, whose letter explained it all

Remnants of the Gothic Line, Borgo a Mozzano

Alessandra Orsini and her uncle Paolo Orsini,
original owners of the villa

With Counsel General Morrison and reenactors

With son Ivan A. at the villa

Photo of WWII Buffalo Soldiers, Bailey Bridge crossing Arno River

CHAPTER 4

2014

I told Mattea Piazzesi that I would visit again in 2014, especially to participate in the seventieth anniversary of the liberation of the city of Lucca. City officials in Lucca learned I was coming and extended an invitation to me to address the city council on September 5, exactly seventy years from the date it was liberated by my regiment of Buffalo Soldiers, the 370th Infantry.

On my way to Lucca in 2014, I thought about my past visits to the battlefields of Tuscany and especially about my visits to the Florence American Cemetery and Memorial. I knew many of the more than four hundred Buffalo Soldiers buried there. Yet here I was, almost ninety years old. I had children, grandchildren, and even great-grandchildren, while the soldiers lay in the soil of Italy, just a memory. I made several speeches that year, both in Italy and in the United States, and I asked people not to forget those young African American soldiers who fought for freedom but whose surviving comrades had not achieved their own freedom in America when they returned from the war and were still subjected to Jim Crow laws. The following poem, which I wrote in 2014, is dedicated to all World War II Buffalo Soldiers, and especially those who are buried at Florence.

With One Tied Hand

Go to Florence
If you will.
See the crosses
Upon the hill.
Notice the murals
On the wall.
Buffaloes in arrows
Represent us all.
Walk the green grass,
Crosses, row on row.
Young Black men
Killed attacking the foe.
It is God who looks
Upon this field.
Blessed men who fought
And would not yield.
Jim Crow was there
Blocking their way.
Causing them grief
Day after day.
These men fought evil
That enveloped the land.
They battled for freedom
With one tied hand.

The poem was well received. I published the poem on bookmarks that I made with Ivan A. and also had it copyrighted. The title of the documentary film we were working on was changed from *The Good Giants* to the same title as my poem, *With One Tied Hand.*

On September 5, the day I was to address the Lucca City Council, I was interviewed at the villa by an Italian journalist who was writing about the seventieth anniversary of the liberation of Lucca. Later that day, I was driven to Lucca and taken to city council chambers. I spoke to the council in English, and Giulia Larturo, the very talented young woman who had translated my book, now translated my speech into Italian for the council members. It was a historic occasion for me and for the citizens of Lucca. We black American soldiers gave the Italians of this part of Tuscany their freedom from the Fascists, and they will always remember that. In 1944, as we liberated towns and villages in Tuscany, we knew the Italians were happy. They showed their emotions with hugs and other demonstrations of affection. I wonder what we would have thought back then if we'd known they would still celebrate their liberation seventy years later with such emotion.

Each of the city council members responded at some length, and the program, which started early in the evening, went well into the night.

On September 6, the author and foreign correspondent Christian Jennings came to the villa and visited with me. Jennings wrote the book *Bosnia's Million Bones,* which is about the vast operation to exhume mass graves and identify the remains of thousands of victims of the 1995 Srebrenica massacre in Bosnia. He was writing a book about World War II in Italy and wanted to interview me. We talked at length about the war in Italy and how brutal conditions were for those of us who did the fighting. We talked about the racially segregated Ninety-Second Infantry Division, my unit, and how we fought alongside soldiers from many different countries and with the Japanese Americans of the 442nd Infantry Regiment. His book, *At War on the Gothic Line*, has now been published.

Later that day, I visited the encampment set up by the reenactors on the grounds of the Villa La Dogana. Again, there were jeeps, trucks, and motorcycles from World War II everywhere. There were rifles, machine guns, and pistols also from the war. For me, it was like going back in time. Everyone wanted to take a picture with me, a Buffalo Soldier who fought there seventy years before. Like last year, the encampment included reenactors as German soldiers in real World War II German uniforms and weapons. I could see the famous machine pistol, what we called the burp gun because the sound it made firing so many bullets so quickly sounded like a series of burps.

Once again, I was asked to sign everything, including helmets and the hoods of jeeps and other vehicles. I saw an M1 rifle, the kind of gun I carried throughout the war, and I attempted to do the "manual of arms," which is how you handle and use weapons while in formation. The gun seemed much heavier after seventy years. During the war, my rifle never left my side. The Garand M1 rifle was the main weapon carried by US infantrymen during World War II. It was semiautomatic and held a clip of eight rounds. When the eighth round was fired, the clip holding the rounds would fly out of the breach. You would reach for another clip with your hand, jam the clip into the breach with your thumb, and pull your thumb out very fast before the breach closed. Some things you never forget!

On September 7, the encampment at the Villa La Dogana was alive with activity as all the reenactors began to prepare for the convoy to Lucca, five miles away. This was the day that the seventieth anniversary of the liberation of Lucca would be reenacted and celebrated. Nearly one hundred men and women dressed in World War II uniforms and carrying World War II weapons, riding trucks, motorcycles, and jeeps, gathered on the large grounds of the villa. After assembling, the convoy of World War II vehicles pulled out and headed for Lucca. Once again, I was in the lead jeep as we rode the five miles from the villa to Lucca. As we reached the city, I could see those famous walls that intrigued me seventy years ago. The walls are 2.6 miles in length, the second longest in Europe, and are of Renaissance origin. The walls are very thick and were designed to stop cannon fire. They also contained bastions for defense.

We entered Lucca and drove to the second-century amphitheater. It is now a piazza with stores, restaurants, and living places. You can still see the arches of the original Roman construction. I got into the sidecar of a World War II motorcycle and was given a brief tour of Lucca, including its World War II museum.

On September 8, I relaxed at the villa. I had enjoyed a very busy schedule, and it was very nice having nothing to do. The next day was very busy. I was interviewed on Italian television, with Giulia Larturo once again helping me as my translator. The interviewer was the same person I'd met at Bagni di Lucca when I visited there in 2012. The white-haired interviewer had been a young boy in an old black-and-white movie about World War II that was shown during our visit to Bagni di Lucca. After this interview, my son and I met Giulia's very beautiful and handsome family. Giulia's mother, father, and younger sisters were present. We then went to the publishing event for the Italian version of my book *Black Warriors I Buffalo Soldiers (e la Liberazione dell'Italia lungo la Linea Gotica)*

The event was held in a large auditorium and was very well attended. The Banca Del Monte di Lucca, Lieutenant Colonel Vittorio Lino Biondi, Professor Umberto Sereni, and Roberto Piazzi e Giulioana Scatena, together with Mattea Piazzesi, had all collaborated with the language department of the University of Pisa to bring about the Italian translation. Giulia Larturo was the translator, and the book was published by Maria Fazzi Editore.

I signed many of the Italian books and wondered why the people in this region of Italy were so interested in what I wrote. I think the fact the Buffalo Soldiers freed them from the Fascists who, under Mussolini, had ruled since 1922 and the Nazis who took over in 1943 was a major reason. Also, I think it was because I wrote about the fighting that took place in the villages, towns, and cities where they now lived. One person said with great enthusiasm, "You mentioned my village in your book. No one ever did that before." Also, I had written about the Gothic Line and our numerous battles against that line of fortifications. I did not know then that the Germans conscripted Italians to build the Gothic Line. People in Italy and tourists still visit its fortifications and can still gather mementoes of those great and small battles where we lost so many young black men.

After the book-signing ceremony, we had dinner under the stars at a restaurant in the Piazza Napoleone, a piazza restored by Napoleon's sister Elisa. It is the main square in Lucca, bordered by a 1500s ducal palace, shops, and cafes. There are cobblestone streets and buildings on each side, set close together. I was with my son, Ivan A., daughter Pam, and her husband, Paul. We drank wine and had a good meal with Mattea and her family. We had had another busy but wonderful day. Our hosts, Mattea

Piazzesi and her husband, Marco Landucci, had a bar in Lucca for a few years and knew almost everyone who passed by.

Mattea's birthday is September 10, and we celebrated at the villa. The birthday was a family event. Mattea's good friends and the friends of Lodovico Landucci, son of Mattea and her husband, Marco, were present for the celebration. My family shared in this festive occasion. We brought presents from Los Angeles just for this special occasion. There was a birthday cake and a special candle brought by my daughter Pam that would not blow out. There were lots of children, and they were having lots of fun with their own games.

On September 11, Solace Wales, the Northern California author, invited my family and our hosts to lunch at her home in the mountaintop village of Sommacolonia. Now home to about thirty people, this village was nearly destroyed when it became the site of a furious battle when German and Italian Fascists attacked an undermanned outpost of Buffalo Soldiers on December 26, 1944. As I have written earlier, it was in this village that artillery officer Lieutenant John Fox, one of only two Buffalo Soldiers to receive the Medal of Honor, was killed in action when he deliberately called for artillery fire on his own position, a forward observation post, after his position was overrun. Fox was from the 366th Infantry.

I think about the sacrifice of Lieutenant John Fox when I read that General Almond, the commanding general of the Ninety-Second Infantry Division, was quoted in 1953, eight years after the war ended, as saying, "The white man is willing to die for patriotic reasons. The Negro is not." This statement is false, of course, and the celebrations and reenactments in Lucca testify to the dedication of Fox and the men like him who fought in the war that December. When General Almond made this statement, hundreds of black soldiers under his command had been killed in action, and many of them are buried in the cemetery in Florence. (The interview and source of the interview are cited in my book *Black Warriors: The Buffalo Soldiers of World War II.*)

The Buffalo Soldiers developed a closeness with the villagers. Solace has written a beautiful book, Braided in Fire: Black GIs and Tuscan Villagers on the Gothic Line, was published in June 2020, about the history of Sommacolonia and the amazing relationship that developed between the villagers and the Buffalo Soldiers caught up in the maelstrom of the December attack. We had luncheon with Solace, her husband, my family, and our hosts. We walked around the mountain village and visited the small but memorable library and museum, which is filled with mementos of the fighting there in December 1944.

There were no planned activities for September 12, but in the afternoon, another group of reenactors came to the villa. Some—both men and women—were from Rome and wore World War II German uniforms. They were present to reenact the liberation of Ponte a Moriano, a city on the Serchio River just north of Lucca.

On September 13, the reenactors' vehicles—and there were a large number—left the villa in a convoy that seemed to stretch for miles and headed toward Ponte a Moriano. Once again, I was in a lead jeep with Mattea Piazzesi and her good friend Tiziana Tosti. Both women were dressed in World War II uniforms of the US Army. I saw that some of the reenactors were in British army uniforms and were carrying bagpipes, while others were dressed as Italian partisans. In other words, the armies and fighting groups that battled in Italy in 1943, 1944, and 1945 were all represented. I thought to myself, *This is going to be a hell of a procession!* As we entered Ponte a Mariano, there was a crowd of both reenactors and other citizens honoring the seventieth anniversary of the liberation of that city.

We drove with the other vehicles around the town square and parked in rows in the square. I got out of my vehicle and walked around looking at the people. There were a large number of reenactors in German uniforms, including some with the apple-green Heer helmets and various German officers. They wanted me to inspect their lineup, and I did. I made a speech to the people, and the reenactors gathered in the square. Giulia Scarpa, once again, translated for me. It was another great event showing how Italy had been affected during the war by Americans, British, Germans, and Italians who fought on both sides of that tragic conflict.

On September 14, I returned to Lucca in order to walk around that wonderful old city. In 2013, the citizens of Lucca had given me books about their city, and I had tried to absorb all of it. I learned about the history and the attractions in the town.

I also wanted to see Il Volto Santo again. I read a great deal about this crucifix, especially after seeing that the figure of Jesus was black and dressed as a king! It has been in Lucca since the year 782.

Once we arrived at the cathedral, I settled into the quiet stillness of the marble chapel. I looked up at Il Volto Santo, said a few prayers, and started to think: When we African American soldiers liberated the city of Lucca on September 5, 1944, during the worst war in the history of the world, we had no idea that in that city there was a black Christ! I took a photo of Il Volto Santo with my iPhone, feeling the need to share this information with many others back home, especially with Deacon Hosea Alexander, a Catholic friend and scholar whom I have known for over fifty years.

After leaving the cathedral, we walked around the city. At a bookstore, I saw copies of my book, published in Italian. Naturally, I had to take a picture. We sat at one of the many outdoor cafes and had refreshments. Many people were strolling through the city. The mayor of Lucca said hello as he walked by. I returned his greeting, happy that this had been another great day. I was learning a little bit more about Lucca and the mystery of Il Volto Santo.

There are several stories about the origin of Il Volto Santo, the Holy Face. One story says it is a thirteenth-century copy of the original, which has been in Lucca since about 1100. I think the story told by Giuseppe Ghilarducci in the book *Lucca Encounters the World,* published in 2009, is my favorite.

According to Ghilarducci, the sculpture is very ancient and is preserved in manuscripts dating as far back as the twelfth century. These manuscripts apparently come from an oral tradition that dates back as far as the ninth century. These manuscripts tell of the discovery of the crucifix in Jerusalem and its amazing journey to Lucca. I planned to learn much more about Il Volto Santo.

On September 15, Mattea, my daughter Pam, and I attended a reception in Lucca. We were invited by Henry DeLuca and his wife, Susan, to their residence. The DeLucas are from Pittsburgh but have close ties to the city of Lucca. The place they were staying was beautiful, but you could never tell that by simply looking at the entrance because you only saw a plain door and walls. Inside the doors and gates, there were beautiful gardens with flowers and olive trees and rooms decorated in a country style or a blend of country and modern. All of Lucca is very interesting in that it is very difficult to tell what beauty lies behind the ancient walls lining the city's narrow streets.

Lucca is an important city because it is included in histories about Hannibal of Carthage, Julius Caesar, and Napoleon Bonaparte. These were important world figures. To me, Lucca is the city liberated by my regiment, the African American 370th Infantry, on September 5, 1944. What makes Lucca stand out is that they have never forgotten the Buffalo Soldiers.

We left for Los Angeles the next day, again carrying memories of people and places that would be with us forever.

At the villa with Fred Kuwornu, Professor Sereni, and translator

Celebrating the liberation of Ponte a Mariano

Inspecting German reenactors

Italian women as reenactors

Reenactors in American and German uniforms

Reenactors in German uniforms at Ponte a Mariano

Signing the hood of a jeep

In the newspaper

CHAPTER 5

2015

Deacon Hosea Alexander and I met during the civil rights struggles of the 1960s. I met with Los Angeles cardinal James McIntyre during this period to ask that the church take a leadership role in bringing about interracial justice. Hosea and I were part of the Los Angeles Catholic Interracial Council, pressing for racial changes in society. When I returned from my visit to Italy in 2014, I took the photo I had taken of Il Volto Santo of Lucca to my friend.

Hosea was impressed both with the crucifix and my reaction to it. He immediately began to study everything he could find about Il Volto Santo. He told me that there were crucifixes of black Jesuses in Caribbean and Central American churches. In many of those countries, the crucifixes of black Jesus are called El Cristo Negro. They all seem to have a likeness to Il Volto Santo, and obviously, all of them appeared in the Caribbean and Central America after 1492. Hosea also found that there were copies of Il Volto Santo in several European cities going back many centuries. Lucca was a major site for pilgrims going to Rome and then to the Holy Land. A section of the pilgrim trail leading to Lucca is called the *Via Volto Santo*. We would hear more about the Via Volto Santo and the Buffalo Soldiers a little later, during my trip in 2016.

I told Deacon Hosea that I would probably return to Italy in 2015, and he asked me to take another photo of Il Volto Santo, looking straight forward with my regular camera. He also gave me a pamphlet showing the crucifix of black Jesus that is in the Cathedral of Our Lady of the Angels in Los Angeles. This larger-than-life crucifix is black and made of bronze and is in the sanctuary. The artist is Simon Toparovsky, who happens to be Jewish. Hosea asked me to please give the pamphlet to the archbishop of Lucca.

I had another goal for my 2015 trip. I wanted to spend some time with Lieutenant Colonel Vittorio Biondi, the Italian army officer who made many of the arrangements for my memorable visit in 2012. Colonel Biondi is a military historian who has written about the Buffalo Soldiers and partisans as they fought the Germans in the December 1944 battle for Sommacolonia.

Finally, I wanted to locate the villa where I had been wounded. I knew it was near the Cinquale Canal and that I could see the Ligurian Sea from its location. After we had captured it, I found a postcard in the villa with a photo of the villa. I went outside, and exploding mortar fire blew me through the front door. A piece of shrapnel stuck in my shoulder. After recovering from the shock of the explosion, I took myself to the medical aid station, which was a field hospital without any of the comfort or conveniences of the hospitals of today. Often these stations were outdoors or in a partially destroyed building, with the cots or beds made from whatever could be found. They separated the wounded into categories, with the more severely wounded transported out. They gave me a shot of tetanus, shook sulfa powder on the wound, bandaged me up, and sent me back to combat. I had kept the postcard and sent a copy to Mattea, asking her if any of her friends knew of its location. Perhaps this time, I would find it.

On September 2, 2015, we left Los Angeles on Alitalia Airlines. Our final stop, once again, was Pisa, and we were met by Mattea and her family. At the villa we met Jan Perry, former Los Angeles councilwoman, and Doug Galanter. Jan, who ran for mayor of Los Angeles, was at that time the general manager of the Los Angeles Economic and Workforce Development Department. Her uncle, William Perry, had been a Buffalo Soldier in my battalion during the war. He served as an adviser to director Spike Lee for his movie *Miracle at St. Anna*. Doug is an attorney. Councilwoman Jan Perry was so interested in the Italian battles of the Buffalo Soldiers, which her uncle frequently talked about, that she arranged for the Spike Lee movie to be shown in the Los Angeles City Council chambers. It was there that I met her uncle in 2010, along with many Japanese Americans, veterans of the 442nd Infantry Regiment who fought alongside us in Italy.

On Saturday, September 5, Vittorrio Biondi came to the villa and picked up my daughter Kathi, my son-in-law Paul, and me. We were on our way to Lucca. Vittorio was now retired from the army. Once we were there, he seemed to know everyone as we walked the streets of that city. We visited San Giusto, a church that had been full of people during the war when a bomb landed on the floor but did not explode. There is now an inscription on the floor where that bomb landed. The inscription reads, "PROIETTILE TEDESCO MIRACOLOSAMENTE INESPLOSO 5-9-1944." Translated into English, it reads, "GERMAN BOMB MIRACULOUSLY DID NOT EXPLODE 9-5-1944. (*Note*: the Italians use the date format of day-month-year.)

Lucca has more than one hundred churches and was a major pilgrim destination in medieval times. We could see trees growing on top of one of Lucca's tallest towers, Torre Guinigi. The soaring medieval brick tower was built by one of the most powerful families in Lucca in the fourteenth century, and the trees grow there because the top of the tower was turned into a garden that included oak trees. We took a casual walk inside those famous walls and enjoyed every moment.

Vittorio took us to his home and introduced us to his wife and three children. We saw them in 2012 but did not really get to meet them. As I have written before, looking from the street, it is impossible to visualize the interior beauty of these living places because on the outside, the buildings look so plain. The insides usually have intricate tile work, gorgeous wood floors, dark woodwork, high ceilings, stonework, and tall windows. These elements all combine to create an elegant but comfortable interior. We had refreshments and then continued our walk to the restaurant, where we would meet Berto Biondi, Vittorio's father. Berto, like me, was ninety years old, and he looked great. I did not know him during the war, though he was a partisan and fought with us. The newspapers covered our meeting with photos and a lengthy article about the Buffalo Soldier and the Italian partisan meeting after seventy-one years. We communicated through Vittorio, who knows some English. Also, I know a little Italian. However, in this setting, much talk was not necessary. Berto and I could understand each other through our gestures and expressions, revealing our feelings of the events that happened so many years ago.

After we had eaten, we walked around Lucca, and then Vittorio took us back to the villa. It had been a memorable day, but it was not over. The Villa La Dogana was filling up with reenactors. Music from the World War II era played, and people were dancing the swing and Lindy Hop. As in the past, all these gatherings at the villa were very festive and happy.

On September 6, riding in World War II jeeps and other vehicles, Mattea and her friend Tiziana Tosti and I went to Borgo a Mozzano, a town north of Lucca along the Serchio River. Along the way, we often saw what is left of the famed Gothic Line, the German defensive line in northern Italy. This line was formidable. Using slave labor, the Germans had created a fortified line with over two thousand machine-gun nests and over four-hundred gun positions, concrete bunkers, observation points, barbed wire, and antitank ditches. Essentially, anything the Germans could do to ensure they had an advantage there, they did, and we once again saw the mountainous terrain, rivers, and streams around these fortifications.

A program was held in the historical center of Borgo a Mozzano, and I learned that I was one of the speakers and an honored guest. I represented one of the last of the African American soldiers who attacked the Gothic Line and helped liberate this part of Italy. I remembered a few things about the Gothic Line fortifications. Our battalion had an antitank platoon, and the gunners told me they fired at the fortifications with their 37-mm cannons. The rounds would hit the fortifications and actually bounce off. It took much larger weapons to break through that steel and concrete.

I did not have a planned speech because I did not know I was on the program until I arrived at the site. When called upon, however, I discussed the difficulties we had in crossing and recrossing the Serchio River and the help we received from the Italian partisans. Mattea translated for me, and I'm certain the audience enjoyed what I said; the fact I was present and had come all the way from Los Angeles was appreciated even more. They were so interested in what I had to say, which was amazing because most of the people present were not soldiers but relatives of the people who lived there during the war. The Italians in that area haven't forgotten, and it means a lot to them that they had help during a time of need. I was followed by an expert who talked about the Italian partisans who had been active in this area and helped us get around many of the fortifications. The final speaker discussed the building of the Gothic Line in this part of Italy. When we finished, we went with a representative of the mayor of Borgo a Mozzano to lay a wreath on the monument for the Italians who died in battle and for the Brazilian soldiers who were attached to the US Fifth Army and occupied Borgo a Mozzano.

Before I left the city, I had another interview with Silvana Galli, author of *Little Blonde*, her story as a young Italian girl who had a child by a Buffalo Soldier during World War II. Earlier in this book, I wrote about Silvana at some length during my visit in 2013, and it was a pleasure to see her again.

On September 8, my daughter Pam and I went with Mattea to visit her horse Cicho. Cicho is kept on a farm in an area with rolling hills several miles from Lucca. There were several other horses kept in old wooden stables on the farm. Many years ago, I rode horses and once rode bareback several miles through the hills in Santa Barbara County. I could see at once how much Mattea cared for her horse. We also went shopping in Lucca and visited one of the many gelato stores.

On September 9, Francesca Fazzi, the publisher of my book in Italian, came to the villa. We talked about the book, which seemed to be doing well in the Italian market. I talked to Francesca about my recent visits and the wonderful reception that I had received. She said she would like to print a second edition, with additional pages describing the reaction by me and by the Italian people to my visits in 2012, 2013, 2014, and 2015. I told Francesca that I thought I could do this, and Mattea said she would help. The Italian second edition of my first book has now been published.

After meeting with Francesca, my daughter Kathi and I went with Mattea to a museum in Brancoli, a small community of about seventy-five people. It includes a parish church, which somewhat distinguishes it from even smaller villages that were common as Tuscany developed. The church is a small and somewhat simple square, gray building with few windows; the front has a tall, dark wooden door in contrast to the light-gray stone. To the left side and right next to the church door is a tall, gray-stone bell tower.

The Linea Gotica Brancoli Association was having a reception, and I was their honored guest. The museum is located at the parish church. Many members of the association were there to greet me. My book and photos of my last visit were in the museum. Brancoli is very close to many of the fortifications of the Gothic Line. It was night when we visited, and we could not see any of the ruins of the fortifications there; it did not take long, however, to see why the Germans built defenses in this location. From these mountains you can see everywhere, yet the rugged and rocky terrain can conceal all activities. We had wonderful refreshments with grateful and friendly people. They were happy to see this one lone Buffalo Soldier after seventy-one years, and I was proud to represent those soldiers who fought in these rugged mountains to give local citizens their freedom.

We seemed to be present whenever Mattea had a birthday, and this year was no exception. It was September 10 again, and her friends gathered for gelato and cake. We are part of her family, and she is part of our family. Once again it was a happy party for a wonderful lady.

I asked Mattea who could contact Italio Castellani, the archbishop of Lucca, to arrange for me to meet with him. Giulio Cesare Artioli, a friend of Mattea's and a reenactor, made these arrangements, and the archbishop met with me, my family, and Mattea's family in the cathedral offices on September 11. Archbishop Castellani was very gracious, and we took pictures and had a brief discussion. He had been in Lucca's city council chambers when I spoke on the seventieth anniversary of the liberation of that city. I told him I was fascinated seeing Il Volto Santo, which we sometimes call the black Jesus, and that I hadn't known of its existence until 2013. I gave him the pamphlet showing the black Jesus in the Cathedral of Our Lady of the Angels in Los Angeles that my friend Deacon Hosea Alexander had given me before I left. Deacon Alexander believes that Il Volto Santo, which came to Lucca in 782, was copied and slowly spread through the Catholic Church in Europe and the Americas. Archbishop Castellani gave me a book, *Vestitio Regis: The Adornment of the Volto Santo.*

Il Volto Santo is a wooden statue of Christ on the cross. Christ is dressed in a plain gown. When I saw Il Volto Santo before the procession on September 13, 2013, Christ was adorned with a golden crown and wore a gown of gold with jewels. He was adorned. The book the archbishop gave me shows how Christ was adorned.

Later that same day, I drove with Mattea to the Cinquale Canal area in another effort to find the villa where I had been wounded. The postcard that I sent with a photo of the villa helped them locate two or three villas that could have been the one where I had been blown through the front door on April 9, 1945, when the Germans, who were in retreat, started shelling us with artillery and mortar fire. We had just captured this villa, where food, ready to eat, was still on the table.

When we reached the canal, I started looking at the villas. The Villa Paoli was at the right place and, although modernized, was probably the one I had been looking for. When I was wounded seventy-one years earlier, I only knew I was at a very large house or villa. Looking at it in modern times, I still was not 100 percent certain that this was the place. There were other large villas nearby, and I strained to see something familiar that would indicate this was the one. I only knew that I was very close. Nothing was exactly the same. The housekeeper was at the gate, and we left a copy of my book with a copy of the postcard photo I picked up in 1945. The owner of the villa later sent me an email showing his interest. He was attending a wedding during our visit, but we would try to meet at some later time. I hoped he could help me find what I was looking for.

On September 12, we drove to Lugnano Vicopisano, which is just north of the Arno River at the place where my battalion crossed, heading north on September 1, 1944. I remembered the area very well. I was in an army vehicle that was fired upon by German 88-mm guns after we crossed the Arno. With me were Private Hiram MacBeth and a driver. MacBeth was asleep when the driver and I dived out of the vehicle as the shelling began. After it stopped, we returned to the vehicle and found MacBeth still sound asleep. Incidentally, I knew it was an 88-mm gun shooting because we heard the explosion before we heard the hiss of the incoming shell, meaning the shell was traveling much faster than the speed of sound. The

Germans' 88-mm gun had a very high velocity, giving it that distinctive sound. It was designed to penetrate the armor of a tank and shoot down airplanes. It was one of the great weapons of the war.

While I was in Lugnano, Vicopisano, many reenactors and civilians took selfies with me and greeted me with enthusiasm and warmth. We went to the city council offices and participated in a news conference. I told those present how we African American soldiers had traveled more than seven thousand miles (eleven thousand kilometers) from the desert in Arizona to reach the Arno River. From my records, we were the first Allied soldiers to cross the Arno. I also told them that African Americans were second-class citizens in our own country during and after World War II and that crossing the Arno River was our first real battle. The people in this community were just happy we had come from so far away.

That evening we had another great dinner at a restaurant near Cerasomma. The restaurant, Il Borghetto del Castello, is located near a castle. When we crossed the Arno on September 1, 1944, the Germans in the stone castle towers in the town of Nozzano could see every move we made as we went north toward Lucca. The village of Ripafratta was nearby.

It rained heavily on Sunday, September 13. We were scheduled to go back to Lugnano, Vicopisano, to see a reenactment, but that event was canceled. We had not heard from the owner of the Villa Paoli, the villa where I was wounded, but Mattea and I decided to drive there anyway. Along the road, from time to time, we saw African women dressed in very colorful outfits, just sitting or standing idly. I told Mattea that these seemed to be "ladies of the night" waiting to be picked up. The rain had stopped, and they smiled, and we smiled as we drove by. The world's oldest profession was still going strong!

We came to the Villa Paoli, and the housekeeper let us in the gate. The owner was still not present, so we were unable to get into the house, but we were able to take a few photos. Remembering what it looked like seventy-one years earlier was difficult; the villa is very close to the Ligurian Sea, however, and I could remember seeing the water after I left the nearby medical station that had been set up in a cellar. Perhaps one day I will be able to return and verify beyond question that this is where I was wounded.

After we returned to the Villa La Dogana, a large group of citizens from Lugnano, Vicopisano, came to visit. Because of the rain, the reenactment of MacBeth and me crossing the Arno and being fired upon in Lugnano, while MacBeth slept, had been canceled. With wonderful kindness, the visitors all brought gifts. I was amazed that this event—with me, the sleeping MacBeth, and our driver—had made such an impression. They had obviously read the story in my book. We took lots of photos and had a great time, but I was very sorry that I could not see the reenactment.

On Monday, September 14, we drove to Lucca and had lunch with Solace Wales. We parked outside the walls and entered the western gate. This is the gate where my battalion stopped in September 1944, the gate where I first saw those wonderful walls. Solace had come from Sommacolonia, and this was our chance to talk about the book she had written and the documentary film I was making based on my book and visits to Italy. Solace and I still have not been able to determine why there are no casualties listed in official army records for the all-black 366th Infantry Regiment.

The restaurant where we ate is outside Lucca's amphitheater. Later, we visited Lucca's cathedral and took additional photos of Il Volto Santo especially for my friend Deacon Hosea Alexander.

The night of the fourteenth, we were invited to the residence of Henry DeLuca and his wife, Susan, for a reception. This year they changed their residence and were living in an apartment that had been built into the amphitheater. Looking out, you could see the oval-shaped piazza of the amphitheater, which is unique because most piazzas are squares. Here, modern apartments and housing have been incorporated into a building that has existed for centuries. The arches that once opened into the amphitheater can still be seen. The slope of the amphitheater has been incorporated in the design of the residences.

After a day of rest, we left for Los Angeles on September 16. At the Pisa International Airport, two American soldiers from nearby Camp Darby recognized me as a World War II veteran. It was easy because I was wearing a cap that said, "Veteran, World War II." Perhaps they had never seen a veteran who fought World War II in Italy because they were quite enthused and wanted their picture taken with me. It was a wonderful way to end a memorable visit.

At Borgo a Mozzano, honoring fallen Italian soldiers

Berto Biondi, who fought with the partisans

Daughter Kathi, Marta, and Mattea at the villa

Family with Lucca's Archbishop Italo Castellani

Italian edition of *Black Warriors* book

Medieval bridge over Serchio River

Silvana Galli, the *Little Blonde*

Speaking at Borgo a Mozzano

CHAPTER 6

2016

When I left Italy in 2015, after my fourth visit in the last four years, I did not think I would return in 2016. I had accomplished many goals and had been treated with extraordinary kindness by the Italians of Tuscany. However, I had not visited the city of Pontremoli, which was liberated by my battalion in the last days of the war and was the site my battalion was holding when the war ended in Italy on May 2, 1945. I still remember that day because the scene in Pontremoli was wild. Guns were going off everywhere, and women who had fraternized with the Germans were seen with their hair cut off to publicly mark these women as German sympathizers. Life wouldn't be easy for them; the Germans were hated. The Italians had been at war since 1940, first on the side of Germany and then switching to the side of the Allies, the United States and Great Britain. Even though much of their country had been destroyed, life could finally return to normal. I had never seen such excitement. It was loud; people were shouting slogans in Italian, celebrating the end of the war. They were hugging and dancing in the streets as people met in restaurants and houses, sharing the news.

Another objective for a trip in 2016 was to finally visit the villa where I had been wounded, but unfortunately, we were unable to contact the owner.

I also wanted to learn more about Il Volto Santo. I had found out that the Holy Face of Lucca (Il Volto Santo) and the Serchio River, which we crossed many times in our battles, are both mentioned in Dante's poem *The Divine Comedy*, written in the fourteenth century. In Dante's poem, the Sacred Face, Il Volto Santo, is described as "black as pitch." This poem is considered one of the greatest works of world literature. This additional bit of intrigue only increased my desire to learn more about the Holy Face.

In Los Angeles, my hometown, I was engaged in many discussions with my friend Deacon Hosea Alexander of the Archdiocese of Los Angeles about Il Volto Santo, the Holy Face, the black crucifix of Christ that is in San Martino, the cathedral of Lucca. Hosea and I discussed the legend of Il Volto Santo on many occasions. According to the legend and popular history, Il Volto Santo was carved by Nicodemus, a disciple of Jesus Christ, after Jesus was crucified. Also according to the legend, Nicodemus wanted people to know what Jesus really looked like. The wood used to carve Il Volto Santo was walnut, and walnut wood is very dark brown. Il Volto Santo arrived in Lucca at a time when statues were being destroyed in the Middle East for religious reasons. We discussed the mystery surrounding Il Volto Santo, its creation, and its arrival in Lucca in the year 782, although some art historians place the origin of Il Volto Santo around the eleventh or twelfth century. There is no dispute, however, that Il Volto Santo is very dark, almost black.

The photos I had taken of Il Volto Santo in 2015 had not included the dove, representing the Holy Ghost, above the head of Christ on the crucifix. I promised Deacon Hosea I would take a proper photo on my next trip to Lucca.

From another source, Mike Mazzaschi, an Italian American who leads tours in Italy, I learned that the photo on the cover of the English-language edition of my book *Black Warriors: The Buffalo Soldiers of World War II* shows African American soldiers of the Ninety-Second Infantry Division advancing toward Pontremoli and the Cisa Pass along a road. That road is called the Via Volto Santo in that part of Italy, but we did not know it at that time. I was determined to find that road and, if possible, the spot where the book cover photo was taken.

It was settled; I would return to Italy in September 2016.

On September 7, 2016, I left Los Angeles with my son, Ivan A., and my daughter Pam and her husband, Paul Chretien. I was wearing my cap that shows I'm a World War II veteran, and people frequently thanked me for my service. I engaged some of the travelers in conversation in the long airport lines and gave them copies of my bookmark, showing how they could order the book I had written. World War II is passing into history, and many did not know there was much fighting in Italy.

We arrived in Rome the next day around noon, waited about two hours, and then took the short flight to Pisa, where we were met by Mattea and her family. We drove to the Villa La Dogana, which had become our home in Italy. The villa remained the same—very comfortable.

We did very little on Friday, September 9, but on Saturday, the tenth, Pam, Paul, Ivan A., and I drove the five miles to Lucca in Paul's rented car. We entered Lucca by its west gate and went inside to a spice shop, Antica Bottega di Prospero, and later went to the Antiche tessiture Lucchesi, where they make their own scarves on an ancient loom. Lucca is a great place to shop and to eat. We saw a bookstore during our walk through Lucca, and my son said he wanted to buy the Italian translation of my book. We went into the store and found the book. The clerk behind the counter in the bookstore recognized me as the author. That was very nice of her and added to the warm feeling that I have toward the Lucchesi people.

When we returned from Lucca, we all knew it was Mattea's birthday, and once again that brought lots of family and friends to the villa to celebrate. We saw Bill Fielders, an American friend who works at nearby Camp Darby as a contract employee. (We met Bill in 2012, and he has been a great friend through all these years.) We brought gifts from the United States just for this occasion. Later that afternoon, professor and translator Giulia Scarpa drove from Florence to join us. Giulia has been of great help in the production of the documentary film being produced from the content of my book and from my recent visits to Italy.

On Sunday, September 11, we drove to Seravezza. With Ivan A. controlling the GPS and Paul controlling the steering wheel, we had very little trouble getting there. Seravezza, the site of a ferocious battle in October 1944, is a small city tucked into the Apuan Alps. Michelangelo found marble there for some of his great artistic works. The marble in the mountains looks like snow when seen from a distance.

My book *Black Warriors: The Buffalo Soldiers of World War II* describes the battle that we fought at Seravezza, and I wanted to see those mountains, streams, and buildings once more. I saw the mountain we captured, held, and finally lost after several German counterattacks. I saw the town of Seravezza at the foot of the mountain; it had been devastated by artillery fire. After running out of ammunition, we were forced down the mountain into Seravezza. During the night after the battle, we were relieved, went into reserve, and began walking through the mountains of Seravezza toward Pietrasanta. We saw a flat green meadow among those mountains, and we stopped for rest. After the battle, it was so peaceful. I always wanted to know where that resting place was. On our maps it was called L'Argentiera (the Silversmiths).

As we drove through Seravezza, I finally found L'Argentiera. It is where the Palazzo Mediceo is located. We were there filming the documentary in 2013, but somehow, I did not recognize the flat area around the Palazzo Mediceo. During the days of battle, we were exhausted from the fighting, and some of us were in battle shock. That peaceful meadow made it seem that we were in another world. Some of us went into a farmer's shed and saw a waterwheel. A farmer was generating electricity with the waterwheel, and a light bulb was lit. We had not seen light from a bulb for many weeks, and we just stared at it in wonder.

At the Palazzo Mediceo, an event was being held, and there were a number of booths on the grounds. We saw Riccardo Biagi, assistant to the former mayor of Seravezza, whom we met in 2013, and he introduced us to the new mayor. We met a number of young people, including Miriam Salvetti and her friend Rachele Colasanti, who were very interested in the history of Seravezza and especially what had happened there seventy years ago during the war. We had a great time with wonderful people.

From Seravezza we drove to Viareggio, past the Cinquale Canal, the site of one of our other major battles, and finally stopped for lunch at the Principe di Piemonte Hotel, which is a large luxury hotel done in classical style. This is the hotel that had been the headquarters of the Ninety-Second Infantry Division during the war. From the rooftop restaurant of the hotel, several miles to the north, we could see Hills X, Y, and Z, the site of many of our battles.

Our goal for Monday, September 12, was to visit Pontremoli, about sixty miles north of Lucca. On the way, we would look for the Via Volto Santo, the road our soldiers took on their way to liberate Pontremoli in the final battle of the war. We found the road and the sign, which said "Via Volto Santo," near a small village called Pontebosio. The sign on the road indicated that it was part of the main pilgrim road, the Via Francigena. The Via Francigena starts in Calais, France, goes through France, then Switzerland, then over the Alps into Italy. The road goes through Lucca and ends in Rome. Visiting Il Volto Santo in Lucca was a major part of the pilgrimage.

My regiment of African American Buffalo Soldiers liberated the city of Lucca, with Il Volto Santo in its cathedral, on September 5, 1944, in our first major battle. In our last major battle, fighting along the Via Volto Santo, we liberated the city of Pontremoli on April 26, 1945. Il Volto Santo, the black Christ, was a part of our history even though we were not aware of its presence.

Battalion headquarters in Pontremoli had been in a building in the center of the city. After we found the Via Volto Santo, we went to the center of Pontremoli and found the building that had been occupied by Third Battalion headquarters at the end of April 1945. This was a two-story building, with a balcony on the second floor overlooking a small town square. I recognized the balcony overlooking this small piazza or square. The sign on the front of the building said *Commune*, or town council. Our battalion commander, Lieutenant Colonel Daugette, did not want to go out onto the balcony to greet the wild crowd when the war ended on May 2, 1945, because there was much shooting. However, he finally did step out and wave to the crowd. He was loudly cheered.

We had lunch across the piazza from the *commune*, and I was recognized as one of the Buffalo Soldiers who liberated Pontremoli. I took pictures with the restaurant owner and his family, and then we drove back to the Villa La Dogana. Another memorable occasion!

Later that same afternoon, Mattea, Pam, Paul, Ivan A., and I went to a meeting at the office of the publisher of the Italian version of *Black Warriors*. There, we met our translator, Giulia Larturo, and Francesca and Maria Pacini Fazzi, owners of the publishing company.

During the meeting I talked about our trip to Pontremoli and finding the road, the Via Volto Santo. I told Francesca about discovering Il Volto Santo in the cathedral in Lucca, taking photos of the crucifix back to Los Angeles, and the reaction I received when I showed them to my friends, especially Hosea. African Americans refer to Il Volto Santo as the black Jesus, while people from Central and South America have a black crucifix of Jesus that they call El Cristo Negro. As I was relating this, Francesca called the publisher of an Italian national newspaper and set up an appointment for me to be interviewed. She thought this was a good story.

As an African American, I was struck by the fact Il Volto Santo was black. A Jesus that was black, like many African Americans, was a surprise and cause for amazement. If the statue of Jesus had been white, I probably would not have taken as much interest in its history. I wanted to know more about Il Volto Santo and where it came from.

I've talked to people about the fact Il Volto Santo is black. To some people, this is not important. To those African Americans who have experienced racial discrimination of some form or another because of their color, Il Volto Santo, the Holy Face, a black Jesus is both wonderful and uplifting.

The fact Lucca, with its black Jesus, had been liberated by black Buffalo Soldiers also made an impact on me. Learning that my regiment was moving along a pilgrim path named the Via Volto Santo added to this wonderful mystery because, in a way, I had discovered a holy path also.

After the meeting with the publisher, we met Giulio Cesare Artoli in Lucca. Giulio is a fireman, a reenactor, and a very good pizza cook. He was arranging for me to join his group during the procession to the cathedral to honor Il Volto Santo the next evening. We had dinner in Lucca and returned to the villa.

Cristiano Consorti, a journalist for *La Nazione*, the national daily newspaper, came to the villa with a cameraman to interview me the next day about Il Volto Santo. The timing was appropriate since it was also the day of the candlelight procession, the Luminaria, through the city of Lucca to the cathedral to honor the holy crucifix. Many would be involved in the procession, including pilgrims from around the world. I was still looking forward to being a part of this event. I told Cristiano Consorti that I had known nothing about Il Volto Santo during the war.

As I continued the interview, I told Cristiano that I had made an enlarged copy of the photo of Il Volto Santo in early 2015 and carried it in a procession with Deacon Hosea

Alexander at Holy Name of Jesus Church in Los Angeles, together with a black crucifix called El Cristo Negro carried by Hispanic parishioners. Holy Name of Jesus is the parish where I became a Catholic and was baptized in 1954. Deacon Hosea thought the facial expression of El Cristo Negro was similar to that of Il Volto Santo.

I also told the journalist that my daughter Kathi, who works with children and young people with problems in the Los Angeles African American community, often gives them copies of the sacred image of Il Volto Santo. Their reaction to seeing a black Jesus is, "Wow." It seems to move them almost as much as it moved me.

The article written by Cristiano Consorti was printed in the September 15, 2016, edition of *La Nazione.*

On September 13, our friend Bill Fielders, from Camp Darby, brought Lieutenant Colonel Crystal Hills, the new commander of the camp, and Master Sergeant Andre Mosby to the villa to meet me. Both are African Americans. I gave Colonel Hills a copy of my book and told her a little bit about my time in Italy during World War II. Colonel Hills gave me one of the army's challenge coins. A challenge coin bears an organization's insignia or emblem and is carried by the organization's members. The coins are usually awarded to prove membership in that organization if a person is challenged to do so and to enhance morale. It was wonderful meeting the officer and the sergeant and thinking how the army had changed during the many years between World War II and the year 2016.

I soon learned that it was going to be impossible to get into Lucca for the procession. Crowds were everywhere, and there would be nowhere to park. I decided to arrange to visit

Il Volto Santo the next day since I had to go to Lucca for lunch with Solace Wales. Solace was coming from her home in Sommacolonia. A museum dedicated to peace is being built in Sommacolonia on the site where the World War II battle took place on December 26, 1944. It will replace a very small museum holding battlefield relics that is currently housed in Sommacolonia.

As we walked through Lucca the next day, we ran into Lieutenant Colonel Vittorio Biondi. Vittorio, who was now retired from the army, had done much for me, especially during the visit in 2012. It was just great meeting him for a few minutes. We met Solace for lunch in an outdoor restaurant adjacent to Lucca's amphitheater. After lunch we went to the cathedral to take proper photos of Il Volto Santo for Deacon Hosea Alexander. The crowds were gone, so I was able to spend some time in the cathedral and thank God for the ninety-one wonderful years of life he has given me. We returned to the villa and started packing. Ivan A. and I were leaving the next day.

But before we left, we met Flavio Grossi, who had ridden his bicycle several miles just to see me before I left for home. He is a good friend and the reenactor who wrote the letter that is printed in this book for the year 2012. It is because of Flavio that I began to understand the deep feeling the Italians of Tuscany have toward the Buffalo Soldiers. Here he was again, expressing that feeling by riding so far just to spend a few minutes seeing me and giving me a hearty embrace. It was wonderful!

After returning to Los Angeles, I made a print of the new photo taken of Il Volto Santo and took it to my friend Deacon Hosea Alexander. Deacon Hosea was very emotional when he saw the black effigy of Christ the King on the cross, with the Holy Ghost (the dove) above his head. As I handed this photo to him, I told him, "Mission accomplished!"

Hosea said, "No, the mission has just started."

Il Volto Santo of Lucca—the black Christ

Inside the walls of Lucca with Ivan A.

Meeting retired Colonel Biondi in Lucca

Meeting with Italian publisher

Pontremoli, where war in Italy ended May 2, 1945

Via Volto Santo, site of our final battle

Buffalo Soldiers in last World War II battle on the Via Volto Santo

World War II Buffalo Soldier return ashes of
Columbus to Genoa, his birthplace, June 1945

CHAPTER 7

2018

I decided to go to Italy in 2018 after not returning in 2017. I planned a return visit to Genoa because my regiment, the 370th, at the request of the partisans we fought with, had asked us to participate in the ceremony on June 6, 1945, returning the ashes of Christopher Columbus to his native city, Genoa. Somewhere in the hills, the partisans had hidden the ashes during the war. The ashes were returned to the Piazza della Vittoria in an ornate urn, carried by a Buffalo Soldier, during a stirring ceremony. My goal this trip was to return to the Piazza della Vittoria.

In addition, I wanted to meet with Liliana, the young Italian woman whom I wrote about who had hidden inside the wall as we fought for the liberation of Lucca. Initially, I told Dr. Janna Merrick, Liliana's friend, that I would probably come to Lucca in 2019 for the seventy-fifth anniversary of its liberation. I learned from Liliana's family and Dr. Merrick, however, that Liliana, now age ninety-six, was dying. Unfortunately, her death occurred before I reached Lucca. Her story of being liberated by the Buffalo Soldiers will always be with me.

I was making plans to return to Lucca in 2019, the seventy-fifth anniversary of the liberation of the city by my regiment in World War II. The Villa La Dogana, where we had stayed each year, was undergoing a change of management and would not be available in 2019. Also, Mattea and her husband had separated. All of this meant my family and I were going to have to look for a place to stay in 2019. After talking with my family, we decided we would stay inside the walls of Lucca when we returned in 2019. We had never done this so it would be a new adventure for all of us. This location would put us in the center of any festivities and celebrations.

I left Los Angeles on September 5. Going with me was my son, Ivan A., and my daughter Pam and her husband, Paul. Pam and Paul have been on every visit, and they make side trips, using the villa as their headquarters.

After a couple of days of rest, Mattea arranged an interview for me on Saturday, September 8, with the local edition of the national newspaper, *La Nazione*. I was interviewed by Paolo Pacini at the Cathedral of San Martino in front of the octagonal chapel of Il Volto Santo. I am called the soldier who liberated Lucca and now the ambassador for Il Volto Santo. I was on the front page of the Lucca edition of *La Nazione*. The article and photos of my visit also occupied most of the second and third pages. While I was being interviewed, a rainbow of light seemed to be shining on me. I was not aware of this, but several people visiting the cathedral, including my son, came over to see what was going on. He took photos, and yes, there is a rainbow of light, and I'm sitting in front of Il Volto Santo. I take this as additional confirmation of something that is so special to me and is connected to the Buffalo Soldiers who fought here and are not forgotten.

On September 10, along with Pam, Paul, and Ivan A., I took the train to Genoa and traveled along a coastal route. There are many small towns and beachfront communities there. The scenery is beautiful. We made it to Genoa in about three hours. The Piazza della Vittoria, where the ashes of Columbus were carried, is very close to the railroad station. We walked, and it took us about twenty minutes to arrive at the piazza. The buildings surrounding the piazza looked the same as they did in 1945. This made recognizing the piazza easy. We took photos, went to a bar for refreshments, and began walking back to the railroad station to catch our train to Lucca. It was a short but enjoyable visit.

Mattea arranged for two of the reenactors, Giulio and Massimo, to come to the villa and discuss their plans for next year, 2019. I wanted to know if there was going to be a celebration of the seventy-fifth anniversary of the liberation of Lucca. Their plans were still in a talking stage at this time. They also discussed forming a Ninety-Second Division Buffalo Soldiers Lucca Association. With no hesitation, I gave them my approval and appreciation for the idea. They promised to keep me updated.

We returned home after a short but eventful visit.

This visit had been a good cause for reflection. My returns to Italy as a World War II African American Buffalo Soldier, beginning in 2012, have been an amazing period of my life, allowing me to reflect more deeply on what our soldiers did for the Italian people and giving me and my family connections in Italy that we cherish.

As my daughter Pam put it:

> We return each year and experience more examples of the respect the Tuscans show to the American Buffalo Soldiers. Our family has been honored by many of the small towns and villages that were liberated. We saw Viareggio, Massa, and the Cinquale Canal. We've met many of the descendants of those who were liberated and listened to their stories.
>
> I made good on my promise to make tacos for Mattea Piazzesi, owner of the Villa Orsini, and I have done so for the past seven years. We now have family there. And they have family here. There is a sense of joy and goodness in all of this.

In 1944 and 1945, as we fought German Nazis and Italian Fascists, we were concerned about our lives. This concern was heightened when we lost friends and outstanding combat leaders. During the war, the only thing we saw that gladdened our hearts were the faces and the hugs and kisses we received from the liberated Italians. We, as black Americans, are their heroes. And now, some seven decades later, we remain their heroes.

Finally, in a very strange and mysterious way, this journey has led to me discovering Il Volto Santo, the Holy Face of Lucca, the black Christ, El Christo Negro. Il Volto Santo has been in Lucca over a thousand years. We Buffalo Soldiers liberated Lucca in 1944, and I first looked upon Il Volto Santo in 2013. The fact our last battle in April 1945 was fought along the Via Volto Santo just reinforces the connections to life and to the people I have encountered as a Buffalo Soldier.

In the Cathedral of San Martino with Il Volto Santo (The Holy Face)

Medieval crossbow procession in Lucca

Return to the site of Columbus's ashes ceremony (1945),
with Ivan A., Pam, and Paul

Buffalo Soldier returning Columbus's ashes in 1945

Lunch in Piazza Napoleone with Ivan A.

El Christo Negro and Il Volto Santo, Holy Name Church, Los Angeles

CHAPTER 8

2019—THE FINAL TRIP

The year 2019 was the seventy-fifth anniversary of the liberation of the city of Lucca by my regiment of Buffalo Soldiers. I talked about this with my son, Ivan A., and daughter Pam while we were still in Lucca. The management of the villa where we had stayed each year was changing. We wanted to stay within the famous walls of that marvelous city. If any activity was to take place, celebrating its liberation, we wanted to be close to the center.

Early in 2019, I developed a serious health issue. My doctors told me that I would have to undergo treatment, but I would still be able to follow a normal living routine. In the late spring, another health issue developed. In 2001, eighteen years ago, I received a quadruple bypass operation. I recovered from that medical issue and had lived a normal life, with proper medication, up until now. I began to have chest pains and was given many different examinations to determine the cause. Finally, an angiogram determined that the quadruple bypass that I'd had in 2001was not fully working. Two of the bypasses were not functioning. At this time in my life, age ninety-four, I could not be surgically treated. I would have to be medically treated. This meant that I could proceed with life as usual but at a slower pace. It also meant that I would go to Lucca, as planned; I would just proceed as a slower pace and not do a lot of planned walking around that wonderful city.

The 2019 trip to Lucca was way beyond all our expectations. We were notified by email and Facebook that the Gothic Line Association of Brancoli was having an event on September 15, the day before we returned to the States. I said we would be present, provided we were given transportation. Brancoli is about a twenty-minute drive from Lucca. Another event was scheduled for the city of Altopascio, which is also near Lucca. Both events were sponsored by the Gothic Line Association, celebrating the liberation events that occurred seventy-five years ago. I was the lone Buffalo Soldier who was able to be present.

Realizing that I did have health issues, I wondered how much walking I should do at Los Angeles International Airport (LAX) and at the airport in Rome. I took a wheelchair to the airplane at LAX. When we landed in Rome, I made a mistake; I decided to walk to the airline connection to Pisa. I had to stop several times and vowed that I would not take that walk again.

Before we left Italy in 2018, we decided to use a rental agency to get us—my entire family, daughters Pam and Kathi, son Ivan, and their spouses, Paul, James, and Leslie—a place to stay inside the walls of Lucca. All of them wanted to be with me in September 2019 when we would celebrate the seventy-fifth anniversary of the liberation of Lucca by the Buffalo Soldiers of World War II. The rental agency came up with a wonderful apartment with six bedrooms, four bathrooms, a very large and comfortable living room, and a kitchen where we could all cook and eat with guests. It looked like the perfect place for the seven of us to live and entertain guests who might drop by for a visit. Also, it was within the walls of Lucca.

Bill Fielders, a friend we met at the Villa La Dogana in 2012 during our first visit, was at the airport to greet us. Bill is a contract employee at the nearby US Army base at Camp Darby. We arranged for a Mercedes-Benz SUV to pick up all seven of us and our luggage at the Pisa airport and take us the fifteen miles to Lucca. We are not little people, and we filled the SUV. We were on our way to Lucca by 4:00 p.m. on September 5.

Automobiles need a special permit to drive into the city of Lucca. The city is completely surrounded by a medieval wall, and the streets are very narrow. The SUV that picked us up from the airport had the special permit and took us from the Pisa airport directly to our new home on Via dell'Angelo Custode.

Our friend Marta Bertani was at our new residence and had stocked the refrigerator with many things we could use. Marta lives and works in Lucca. On all our prior visits, she helped Mattea Piazzesi manage the Villa La Dogana, where we were staying. Also, Marta had visited Los Angeles in 2018. She stayed with my daughter Pam. The whole family pitched in with social events and some entertainment. Her visit was enjoyable for all of us. I showed Marta the Pacific Ocean, although unfortunately, it was a rather foggy day.

Dr. Robert Darryl Banks, OBE (Order of the British Empire), and his son David arrived the same day as we did. They were staying at a hotel in Lucca, and I told them to come by for a visit. Dr. Banks's father was a Buffalo Soldier, a member of the 317th Medical Battalion that supported the 92nd Infantry Division. In other words, Dr. Banks's father was a combat medic. He contacted me after reading my book and came to Los Angeles in the spring of 2019, while he was visiting his son in San Francisco. Dr. Banks is a Rhodes Scholar and was awarded the OBE for work he did that increased scholarship opportunities for black students in Great Britain. He now runs his own consulting firm and is a distinguished scientist and environmental and energy policy expert. He and his son, who lives in San Francisco, were keenly interested in the events surrounding the liberation of Lucca by the Buffalo Soldiers seventy-five years ago.

Also joining us for a few days in Lucca was James Maddox, a Vietnam veteran, and his wife, Natalie. James was a former National Service Officer for one of the veterans' organizations and is keenly interested in the story of the Buffalo Soldiers. My son's friends Jimmy and Jeannie Jackson helped fill the contingent of folks interested in both Lucca and the return of the Buffalo Soldier.

On Friday, the day after our arrival, I was invited to a coffee-and-ice-cream reception by the family of Liliana of Lucca. Liliana was in her early twenties when the Buffalo Soldiers of my regiment liberated the city. (I described these events in the last chapter.) As I mentioned, Liliana died just before I arrived in Lucca in 2018. She had seen my picture and thought I was the soldier who found her asleep, woke her up, and told her that Lucca was liberated and she was free.

I told Dr. Janna Merrick, Liliana's friend for several years, that my family and two friends were with me, and all nine of us needed transportation to the party. Transportation was arranged by Liliana's family, and we were picked up by three automobiles near the ancient walls of the city and taken to the home of Liliana's daughter. The daughter's home is modern and is outside the walls of the city. I met Dr. Janna Merrick for the first time. We had been emailing each other for over two years.

Many family members and friends were present at Liliana's daughter's home. One granddaughter, Alessia, speaks excellent English and is a friend on Facebook. Alessia was of great help to those of us who did not speak Italian. One older man was a young boy when the Germans occupied Italy. He spoke vividly of the atrocities committed by Nazi soldiers. I made a few remarks, telling them where I came from and that I did not enter Lucca on September 5, 1944, the day of its liberation. I was with my battalion, looking at those famous walls and admiring what I could see of the buildings inside.

The party lasted a few hours, and we were all full of ice cream and wonderful pastries when we were taken back to our residence in Lucca. It had been a wonderful day with very grateful people. One of the partygoers said Liliana said the people of Lucca danced all night with the Buffalo Soldiers when they were liberated.

The next day, September 7, I was asked to come to the city of Altopascio, a community about fifteen miles east of Lucca. The reenactors from the Gothic Line Association were there with their World War II guns and vehicles. It was the celebration of the liberation of that community by the Buffalo Soldiers, seventy-five years ago. I was an honored guest. Ivan A., Kathi, James, and I were picked up by our wonderful friend and the owner of the Villa La Dogana, Mattea Piazzesi, and driven to the event in Altopascio.

At Altopascio, I was given an American flag and a certificate explaining the reason for the gift. The certificate reads as follows:

The Flag
of the
United States
of America

This is to certify that the accompanying flag was flown over the Florence American Cemetery on September 6, 2019 for

Ivan J. Houston

In honor of our visit during the 75th anniversary ceremony of the liberation of Altopascio, Italy

Angel M. Matos
Superintendent

This was a great honor for me. I have visited the Florence American Cemetery several times, and I've always noticed the American flag flying over that beautiful yet solemn place.

The final honor given to me at Altopascio came from the mayor of that city, Sara D'Ambrosia (born in 1987), who spoke passionately about the Buffalo Soldiers who liberated them. I was also given a plaque from Camp Darby, the huge US military supply base that is nearby. The Linea Gotica Della Lucchesia (the Gothic Line Association of Lucchesia) gave me a plaque for participating in the seventy-fifth anniversary of the liberation of Altopascio. Altopascio is just north of Pontedera, where many Buffalo Soldiers of my regiment crossed the Arno River, battling their way toward Lucca and the Gothic Line.

Once again, I was proud to represent the Buffalo Soldiers who fought long ago to liberate this beautiful part of Tuscany.

I felt we could rest on Sunday, September 8, but the reenactors wanted us to return to Altopascio for additional honors. Once again, Mattea picked us up and took us to Altopascio. We were given honors again, but much of the program was about the role the Brazilian Expeditionary Force. We fought alongside the Brazilians, and we Buffalo Soldiers all noted that they were integrated, while we were still fighting in a racially segregated army. I remember when our battalion was replaced by a Brazilian battalion during combat in the Serchio Valley. The two battalion commanders could not understand each other—one spoke English, and the other spoke Portuguese which is the national language of Brazil. My company commander, Captain Shires, said, "Get Corporal Houston; he knows Spanish and can help us." I guess Shires found out I'd studied Spanish in college. The Brazilian commander knew a little Spanish and a little Italian. By that time, I knew a little Italian in addition to a little college Spanish. We talked back and forth and finally came to an understanding. The Brazilians were able to replace our battalion in proper order.

The next day, we had a visit from Lieutenant Colonel Vittorio Biondi, now retired from the Italian army. Vittorio has been our friend since our first visit. As described earlier, the success of our initial trip was largely due to his organization. Vittorio and his family live in Lucca very close to where we were staying. Vittorio visited us, along with Carlo Pudu, an excellent translator who works closely with the mayor of Lucca, and Ilaria Vietina, who also works closely with the mayor. Our visit with Mayor Alessandro Tambellini was now scheduled for the next day, September 10. Vittorio invited the entire family to dinner that night at an excellent restaurant, which was just a few blocks from where we were staying.

September 10 was our scheduled meeting with Mayor Tambellini. His office was just a short distance from where we were staying. Colonel Biondi picked me up and drove me in his BMW to the mayor's office. Our friends the Maddoxes were able to come with us for this historical meeting celebrating the seventy-fifth anniversary of the liberation of Lucca. I didn't know what kind of meeting was going to take place as we sat in the mayor's waiting room.

At noon, the mayor's office door opened, and all nine of us were escorted into the office of Mayor Tambellini. The beautiful room was white and decorated with gold paint. The mayor said real gold was used in the decoration. There was a circle of chairs for my family and the Maddoxes; the mayor; Carlo Pudu, who served as translator; Ilaria Vietina; and Paolo Pacini, the journalist and photographer who recorded this event for the media and for history.

I gave the mayor a copy of my book *Black Warriors: The Buffalo Soldiers of World War II* and described how the Buffalo Soldiers crossed the Arno River and liberated the city on September 5, 1944. I told him we faced fierce fighting on the outskirts of Lucca, especially in a village called Ripafratta. When soldiers of our Second Battalion entered the city, however, all was calm. As a soldier in the Third Battalion, I saw the city from the west gate but did not enter.

The mayor then gave me gifts, including a medallion of the city of Lucca. I was quite honored. We then lined up for photos in this beautiful, ornate room. Paolo Orsini took the photos, and the very next day, this photo of me and my family

(Paul and Pam Houston Chretien, James and Kathi Houston Berryman, Ivan A. and Leslie Jackson Houston), along with Mayor Alessandro Tambellini and Ilaria Vietina, appeared on the front page of the Lucca section of the national news.

The Sacred Face of Lucca, Black Jesus
Il Volto Santo

Come to Lucca,
Look behind its wall.

See ancient churches
Count them all.

Notice the cathedral
its sculptured face.

Hidden inside
The black Holy Face.

Il Volto Santo
The Italians say.

Sculpted by Nicodemus
In a holy way.

Pilgrims came to see
From a distant land.

To visit the crucifix
Held sacred by man.

Centuries past
His eyes saw it all,

They encouraged
Man's innocence
Before the fall.

War clouds gathered, hatred began.
Destroying freedom held sacred by man.

Bombs from the sky
Tanks began to rumble.

Ancient walls threatened
Some began to crumble.

In Lucca, behind its walls it stood.
Its Face showed man is misunderstood.

The Face was Christ crucified for humanity,
Who rose again to crush man's insanity.

Through all this chaos
There came relief.

Black soldiers fought their way
Showing holy belief.

They died to liberate that Holy Face
To show that man is still in God's grace.

Ivan J. Houston
August 18, 2018 (rev.)

Author Ivan J. Houston with Alessandro Tambellini,
mayor of Lucca, in front of Il Volto Santo

Author Ivan J. Houston with Francesca Fusaro (the Hugger)

Author Ivan J. Houston with Linea Gotica
Brancoli Reenactors, Brancoli Museum

Documentary poster for Lucca showing

Festival of Lights in Lucca

The family, Ilaria Vietina, Historian of Lucca, and
Mayor Alessandro Tambellini of Lucca

WWII jeep signed by author Ivan J. Houston and
Medal of Honor recipient Vernon Baker

AFTERWORD
(IN THEIR OWN WORDS)

We have included some remarks from some of the people who meant so much to Dad on his many trips to Italy. One of the final highlights was my (Ivan A.'s) return visit in 2022. We donated items that also included a section of a map with the city of Pontremoli circled. That is where Dad was when the war ended. Also included was a letter to his mother, Doris, along with a number of personal WWII items, which are on display at the Museum of the Memory of Brancoli in the part of the WWII museum dedicated to Ivan J. Houston.

> The Room of the Allied Forces' Ivan J. Houston Named after the sergeant of the Ninety-Second Buffalo Division who, as a young man, liberated the Serchio Valley with the other African American soldiers of the Buffalo Division. Ivan J. Houston, after seventy years, returned to these areas and discovered how much he was still loved by the Italians who were liberated by the Buffalo Soldiers.

Author's letter to his mother, 1945

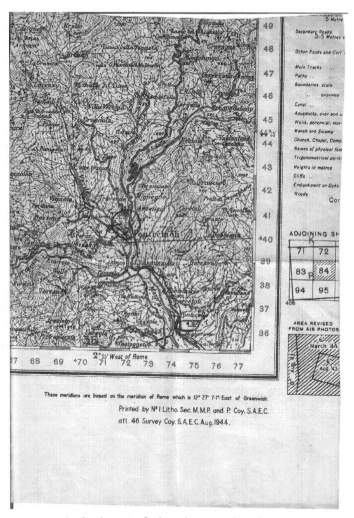

Author's map of where he was when the war
ended, circled Pontremoli Italy

Viareggio, Italy
Oct. 12, 1945

Dear Mother:

How are you? I am still well, happy and wondering if I'll make it home within the next few weeks. So far, so good!!

The mail does act strangely at times and I am sorry you did not hear from me for three weeks. I do write you at least once a week despite any circumstances that may arise.

I have no new new experiences to bring forth and as usual everything has been pretty much in a state of confusion as we prepare to move to the staging area. The weather, which nearly approached freezing, has warmed up quite a bit. We are still living in tents and cold weather is definitely not appreciated.

You say Norman has only about 58 points? This is very damaging since he came into the Army 1 year before me and, according to the latest count I have 61 points. I have

Author's letter to his mother, page 1

been recommended for the Bronze Star for Heroic Achievement in action about 1 year ago. I saved to soldiers who were wounded and carried them through the shelling to the aid station. I don't know if I'll get this medal tho since it was such a long time ago that the incident occurred.

You say you don't know whether or not I received the 60 dollar money order. I did.

Enclosed is a section of a map with the city of Pontremoli' encircled. I was there when the war ended — save if for my scrap book. I have also sent a number of other maps and the history of the 92nd Division to you. They should prove interesting.

Love,
Dan

P.S. I will keep you posted on my status.

Author's letter to his mother, page 2

Ivan A. and Leslie Houston, with Francesca Fusaro at
Brancoli Museum room dedication for Ivan J. Houston

FLAVIO GROSSI
REENACTOR

Eternal Gratitude

"Eternal gratitude" … beautiful words!

When I was a kid (we are talking about almost fifty years ago, twenty years after World War II ended), our favorite pastimes were—like most kids back then—soccer, hide-and-seek, and war games with wooden rifles and pistols made by our fathers. Also, we loved to play with toy soldiers in endless battles we used to create with our imagination.

Sometimes my father—and my grandpa too—told me war stories. I was fascinated by those tales of soldiers who came from far away to free us from the Germans.

Our teacher at the elementary school made us sing "Bella ciao," or "Glory, glory, hallelujah," a song about John Brown, whose body "lies a-moldering in the grave." In my head, I imagined John Brown as an American soldier who came from so far away and died to give us liberty!

Eternal gratitude is the feeling that today I have for all those soldiers who freed us!

MY HEROES

Back then, my heroes were American soldiers carrying the flag with stars and stripes as a symbol of their identity. My dream was the American helmet; how beautiful it was! Once, my dad took me to one of his friends. I don't remember his name, but I remember that, after welcoming me, we went down into his cellar.

When he opened the door, I was fascinated by what I saw before my eyes—a lot of stuff (mostly American) showing the print "US." I immediately asked my father what that meant, and he said, "The United States." Meanwhile, his friend, who was turning his back, came to me with a helmet in his hands— the American helmet!

Beautiful!

I was speechless, and I was scared to even touch it! He kindly handed it to me. It was so heavy. I asked him if I could wear it, and both he and my father nodded.

At that very moment, I was the happiest kid on earth! Two things I remember about that helmet: the name of the soldier that was written inside and the state from where he came (only when I was older, because of my studies, did I understand it was one of the fifty states of the Union), and a coat of arms. I thought it represented a buffalo, so I timidly asked my father's friend for an explanation. He said very politely, "Son, this helmet belonged to an American soldier from the Ninety-Second Buffalo Division!"

During the following days, I asked my father who those soldiers were. And yes, I saw them in person. At that time when they arrived and marched through our valleys, I was only six years old. My father remembered them too, and while he was telling this story, those memories brought back some sort of joy because the soldiers carried with them food—like, a lot of food—and especially freedom!

My father used to call them *mori* because they had black skin, Afro Americans. Today, he remembers them with the same word, but there is another expression that I will never forget: *good giants.*

My father used to call them that way because he told me they gave him chocolate all the time, lots of bread, canned food, powdered milk, and cigarettes for my grandpa, Pietro. Well, in my father's eyes, they were very tall men, big, and gentle: good giants!

Unforgettable Memories

With years passing by, those beautiful moments of my childhood were replaced by my adolescence. Inside me, the admiration I had for the United States of America didn't change a bit and caused me to spend my honeymoon in that immense world called America. Only when my father and I saw the movie *Saving Private Ryan* were all those under-the-ashes memories brought back vividly. Coming out of the movie theater, we looked at one another, and he promised that one day we would go to Normandy. That happened in May 2011; it was an incredible experience!

Meanwhile, my passion for World War II made me join a group for historical reenactments in Lucca, the Linea Gotica della Lucchesia, and it was exactly through this group that I had the opportunity to meet my good giant, Ivan J. Houston, a veteran from the Ninety-Second Buffalo Division. He decided to stay with his relatives, where he had stayed seventy years before, at Villa la Dogana in Cerasomma near Lucca. Thanks to Mattea Piazzesi, the owner of the villa, and to the group Linea Gotica della Lucchesia, we were able to organize a wonderful welcome ceremony for Ivan. Very emotional! Incredible!

Then I decided to write a letter to Ivan so that I could express my eternal gratitude for all those soldiers who came from far away to give us freedom.

From that day on, I had a special friendship with Ivan, and it grew through many different occasions. A documentary about the American military cemetery in Impruneta, near Florence, was shot. My letter was read in a scene of the documentary, while I was wearing the military uniform that the American soldiers used to wear! Every time that Ivan and his family went back to America, to California, I felt it was a "see you soon," not a goodbye, and indeed, he used to come back to Lucca almost annually.

Later, I became part of the board of the group Linea Gotica di Brancoli, and I worked with incredible people, very passionate and motivated, to save all the memories of the war from oblivion. A beautiful museum in the small village of San Giusto di Brancoli, near Lucca, was opened and became part of a series of sights, including many German bunkers built on this side of the Linea Gotica.

We dedicated one of the rooms of the museum to Ivan J. Houston, the one about the Allied Forces. A plate on the wall will forever remember our gratitude to him and all the soldiers who freed us.

I am proudly part of this group and thank the efforts of everybody, including my friend Piergiorgio Romboli, who prematurely passed away. We were able to bring back the American veteran Ivan, who visited Ponte Mariano and San Giusto di Brancoli, two places where he fought. The best memory I have is the day of his arrival in San Giusto di Brancoli, with bells tolling and people in the streets singing "Glory, glory, hallelujah!" When he arrived in a jeep, a car that was made available by the group Linea Gotica della Lucchesia, we escorted him to the front of the church in the village square, where more celebrations took place.

How emotional! My last memory of Ivan is a picture of me and him hugging my father. I get chills just thinking of it.

Unforgettable memories, memories of moments that were possible thanks to extraordinary men and incredible human beings who, with their passion, made all of this possible!

Eternal gratitude to all the boys who died to grant us liberty. Eternal gratitude to those who, from eighty years ago to today, remember the sacrifice to achieve a life in peace. Eternal gratitude to my father, my mother, and my family, as they educated me with these values. Eternal gratitude to my wife, who made me a better man. Eternal gratitude to all my true friends, to those I felt close to me, especially during hard times. Eternal gratitude for those who worked to keep alive all these memories and memorabilia, eternal gratitude to the group Linea Gotica di Brancoli. They rescued all the stories of our beloved, who will be remembered during the years to come.

And eternal gratitude to you, Ivan J. Houston, the good giant.

MATTEA PIAZZESI
OWNER, VILLA LA DOGANA, LUCCA

I'm a never-ending talker, but I'm not able to describe feelings. When I think about Ivan, my feelings are endearment and gratitude. Through Ivan, I learned many things regarding Italian and United States history. It made me go deeper into both cultures—how people acted during and after WWII. It has been more real, touchable, than what we study at school or watch on TV.

Since I watched him on a YouTube video presenting his book at UCLA, I felt he was an outstanding person. He had such an energy! Once, we went to Sommocolonia, and he was hiking next to me very naturally, but he said he didn't feel that strong. Then I learned he had a surgery back in US to resolve the reason he was weaker.

I loved greeting him at every event that was organized for his arrival, each year when he came back, and I loved our emailing during his book translation, writing to him, always getting an immediate and accurate response at any hour of the day or the night.

I loved being a part of the documentary production, scouting places that he'd indicated and finding those who were there during that period. He was always on the ball, definitely. He was outstanding!

It seemed to me that he felt grateful for life, and he wanted to honor all the other silent soldiers who lost their lives fighting and to illuminate the discrimination they suffered. Reading the book and knowing him, I found he was an extremely dignified, elegant man and seemed to be at peace with those deemed "first class," much like an adult who's amused by a child putting on airs.

He used to come back for my birthday that is close to the Settembre Lucchese events, and we used to party, both families together becoming a single one. This has been the last times I celebrated it.

The first time he came, he gave me a present, which was, according to his family, a cameo he talks about in his book. I was stunned by it. To me, it meant so much! Also, the fact his daughters, Pam and Kathi, and son, Ivan A., were glad about it made me feel part of the family. Every year, he came with a family present.

He was special!

MARCO LANDUCCI
SWIMMING COACH

I would like to make you understand why Mr. Ivan represented a symbol for me, and I will try starting from childhood memories that I always have alive in my mind.

In my family, memories of moments lived during the Second World War often came out. I speak of the 70 years, and my parents and grandparents had lived it to the fullest. Also, my house was used first by the Germans and then by the Americans, as a place of command. But these were only abstract memories. But it happened that everything materialized when, one year, a gentleman showed up at the gate of the house, asking—with gestures and in a "strange" language—for my father and my grandfather. I called them, and there was a great chaos, hugs, tears, and rounds of phone calls that anticipated the arrival of relatives and friends—and again, hugs and tears. I didn't understand much. I was about ten years old, but it was very exciting.

They explained to me later that he was a former American soldier who had been in my house after the liberation of Lucca and that he was touring the places where he had been during the war. A short time later, I was in a house where we went for the summer holidays, which belonged to my maternal grandparents, in a town called Capezzano, or a few kilometers from Sant'Anna di Stazzema, unfortunately famous.

Same scene—crying, hugs, and so on. He was another ex-military! I have a pleasant memory of this because he spent a lot of time with me and my cousins, all between eight and ten years old, making drawings and teaching us how to make paper objects such as airplanes, ships, and more. I never knew why he wanted to be with us children because when I asked my mother and my aunts, they began to cry. I think it was linked to Sant'Anna di Stazzema because the next day, they wanted to go there. That began many stories of those facts that would be in the public domain many years later.

Two very elegant people in their way, gentlemen, but they did not make me think of the soldiers—those with whom I played, the toy soldiers with whom I reproduced the events based on family memories.

I understood that they were people like my grandparents, who had families and normal lives, and this seemed strange to me, that from so far away, they had come to free us, fighting to ensure democratic freedom.

So many years went by, and I didn't think it could happen again. But I was no longer a child.

I couldn't let a person I have in my memories just show up at the gate. And so I set off to ensure that the welcome would be worthy. With the help of many, we have managed to do everything that has been done.

I have only one regret for Ivan—not being able to communicate all my joy at knowing him. It was enough for me to hear him speak, at home and in official meetings where translators were present, to be able to accompany him by car from one place to another, but I realize that something was missing. I wanted to do more. And anyone who knew Mr. Ivan knows why I say that.

Proud to have known him and his whole family.

FRANCESCA FUSARO
BRANCOLI GOTHIC LINE COMMITTEE
REENACTOR, HISTORICAL GUIDE, HUGGER

"In remembrance of his birthday and in honor of an amazing man today I want to tell you about Ivan J. Houston, sergeant of the Ninety-Second Infantry Division, Buffalo, the only black unit to see combat during World War II. Here in Tuscany, they are often called the *mori* (Moor). I first met Ivan during the historical reenactment of the seventieth anniversary of the liberation of Lucca. I saw it at Ponte in Moriano, and it was a great emotion. My heart was beating fast to see that nice group of close and passionate reenactors, men and women in their beautiful uniforms, all composed and concentrated in waiting for this man and enrapt, presenting the events of those distant days—the German retreat and the American advance.

At some point in time—here it is! Ivan aboard a Willis, met by long, warm applause and even a few tears, mostly from older people. African American, a sergeant. One of the many, many black kids who crossed an ocean to help the Italian people.

Here it is! He's here, flesh and bone. Honoring all those who didn't make it. During his visit, he presented his book *The Black Warriors*; getting closer—there was a lot of fight. With my book, I wanted an autograph and to shake his hand. Magic! I got very emotional, and I thanked him, thinking that if I was there, it was also because of him and men like him.

Ivan was born today, but in 1944, he was a student at the University of Berkeley in California. He was good at school and, above all, an athlete—he was also a boxer. In fact, he has maintained a massive and important physical appearance as an grown-up. I'd say it wasn't necessary to punch him!

The Events

America officially goes into war, with all its power in arms and men, after the attack on Pearl Harbor; hard one to swallow! From there, a long series of events lead Ivan and other guys like him to board a ship at the age of nineteen. The journey has been long and tough. He has crossed an ocean.

Italy

Ivan had just made history. Then he became a sergeant in the only division of black men, the Ninety-Second Infantry Division, Buffalo.

"We, for Italians, were of 'first level'; we were heroes."

Disembark in Naples—obviously, the war had left deep wounds, and it didn't look good at all, on the contrary! Here, he began to realize what had happened, and he had compassion above all for the population. From Naples and with the various means of transport and sections in gear, slowly it reaches our area with its companions—Pontedera, Pisa, Viareggio, Barga, Massa, Lucca.

Objective: Break the Gothic Line

September 1944, Lucca is liberated!

A very young Ivan waits outside of the walled city. He is unable to enter then, but a seed is planted. The seed grows over the decades, and he finally returns to pass through the gates and enter the city of Lucca.

Ivan's book is basically a diary; in fact, he daily listed the various movements that the division made. What struck me, among many very technical and detailed events, was when he talked about the weather they found in September with us—rain and the Serchio River getting bigger. Fighting intensified; the number of deaths increased; so did the vigil hours!

They were at war, and among everything, it became difficult to wash, change the uniform, eat a little, quiet, but socks! Yeah right, those—whole weeks in those boots with the same pair of socks, poor things! The captain then gave the order: "Change socks!" Trench foot would have become a big problem.

He also writes, "We were so nervous young people, but I didn't feel afraid. I was about to start a great adventure. I didn't think I would be hurt or die."

Only hardened men and women could stand war and a life of so much sacrifice.

Ivan, like all the soldiers who came to Italy, had to face considerable sacrifices. The only positive thing was that in terms of equipment, he didn't lack anything.

The population of Italy remembers chocolate, candy, cigarettes, and aid of various kinds. Witnesses of these events, who are over-age, to this day shed tears as they remember them; in our part, they were called "the mori"!

They have seen the horrors of war, and many, many are buried in the Florence cemetery.

I invite you to read his book. You will understand many reasons; one is the connection with Italy. Ivan felt loved and appreciated here. In his country, America, there was still strong racism, and unfortunately, even when he came back, it didn't change much.

War is over, and we are coming home. The adventure is over!

"On the evening of December 5, I took a train … it was almost midnight when I rang the doorbell: my mom and grandma opened the door. I am home."

In Lucca, in September 2019, at Palazzo San Micheletto, Ivan is presenting his documentary/video about the war (*With One Tied Hand*). The room was packed, and no one was breathing. There, at the end of the documentary, was a very long applause—a beautiful emotion.

After various meetings in the city on September 15, it's our turn for the committee! Ivan and his family honored us by coming to Brancoli and visiting the museum and the areas where the Gothic Line was built.

All the family and friends got on board the jeeps to wait for them and to give them the right tribute to the Church of San Giusto di Brancoli. There were revolvers, flags, and many people, all accompanied by a background of music suitable for the occasion.

Following was a series of tributes, testimonies, commemorations, and thanks that will remain imprinted in the memories of those who were present that day.

Our goal was to make Ivan feel at home, like seventy-five years ago, but without war! To top it off, we wanted to pay homage by hosting a lunch with lots of local goodies that we knew would be appreciated by these guests who came from far away.

It Was the Last One

Unfortunately, Ivan, in a clinic in Los Angeles, on March 1, 2020, closed his eyes at the age of ninety-four years old.

The sorrow was great for many of us. The short time and the difficulty of the language prevented us from spending hours and hours with him, but we are content and cherish those few minutes, a greeting, a word, a photo, a handshake.

Together with him, we became part of his story for the last time. We all have become his people.

What did his visit leave me with? A hug, asked in front of a crowded room, in total embarrassment. A strong hug, emotional, of pure history, made of heroes, of strength, of courage and thankfulness—a meeting between two generations, very different and very far apart.

Sending a hug—that time it was me and him. In the background ... a loud and long applause.

Ivan, we thank you and honor you with the same words of the license plate that we, as the committee, donated to you on the day of the event. Do you remember?

YOU CROSSED AN OCEAN WITHOUT FEAR.

Happy birthday, Sergeant Ivan J. Houston, wherever you are.

Printed in the United States
by Baker & Taylor Publisher Services